MUSIC

by Ted Greenwald

Series developed by Peggy Schmidt

Princeton, New Jersey

A New Century Communications Book

Other titles in
this series include:

CARS
COMPUTERS
FASHION
FITNESS
HEALTH CARE

Greenwald, Ted, 1959–
    Music / by Ted Greenwald.
        p.   cm.—(Careers without college)
    "A New Century Communications book."
    Includes bibliographical references.
    ISBN 1-56079-219-1 (pbk.) : $7.95
        1. Music trade—Vocational guidance—United States.
2. Music—Economic aspects.   I. Title.   II. Series.
ML3790.G76   1992
780′.23′73—dc20

92-31320
CIP
MN

Art direction: Linda Huber
Cover and interior design: Greg Wozney Design, Inc.
Cover photo: Bryce Flynn Photography
Composition: Bookworks Plus
Printed in the United States of America
10   9   8   7

Text Photo Credits
Color photo graphics: J. Gerard Smith Photography
Page xiii:
  Sinead O'Connor: © Kate Garner
  Hammer: © Annie Leibowitz
  Garth Brooks: © Beverly Parker
Page xiv: © Reuters/Bettmann
Page 18: © The Bettmann Archive
Page 36: © The Stock Market, Inc./Mark M. Lawrence
Page 54: © Michele Taylor Photography
Page 70: © The Stock Market, Inc./Lee L. Waldman

ABOUT THIS SERIES

Careers without College is designed to help those who don't have a four-year college degree (and don't plan on getting one any time soon) find a career that fits their interests, talents and personalities. It's for you if you're about to choose your career—or if you're planning to change careers and don't want to invest a lot of time or money in more education or training, at least not right at the start.

Some of the jobs featured do require an associate degree; others only require on-the-job training that may take a year, some months or only a few weeks. In today's real world, with its increasingly competitive job market, you may want to eventually consider getting a two- or maybe a four-year college degree in order to move up in the world.

Careers without College has up-to-date information that comes from extensive interviews with experts in each field. It's fresh, it's exciting, and it's easy to read. Plus, each book gives you something unique: an insider look at the featured jobs through interviews with people who work in them now.

Peggy Schmidt

ACKNOWLEDGMENTS

Many thanks to the following people who provided their invaluable assistance:

Tommy Casassa, Studio Manager, Masterlink Studios, Nashville, Tennessee

Lainie Fraser, Studio Manager, The Production Block, Austin, Texas

Terry Fryer, President, Fryer Music, Chicago, Illinois

Dave Gannon, Engineer, Rocky Mountain Recorders, Denver, Colorado

Shirley Kaye, Executive Director, SPARS, Lake Worth, Florida

Dan Klaiber, Senior Engineer, Audiocraft, Cincinnati, Ohio

Paul Lehrman, President, Lehrman Productions, Arlington, Massachusetts

Paul Lonnegren, Communications Coordinator, NAMM, Carlsbad, California

Jeanne McGrail, Studio Manager, Soundtrack Recording, Boston, Massachusetts

Dominic Milano, Editor, *Keyboard Magazine*, Cupertino, California

Leslie Morgan, Corporate Relations Assistant, BMI, New York, New York

Marilyn Morgeson, Studio Manager, Studio A Recording, Detroit, Michigan

Jas Obrecht, Associate Editor, *Guitar Player Magazine*, San Francisco, California

Myron Partman, Studio Manager, Ironweed Studios, Seattle, Washington

Chris Plunkett, Exhibits Manager, AES, New York, New York

Shawn Rae, Orchid Communications, Paramus, New Jersey

Matt Resnicoff, Associate Editor, *Musician* magazine, New York, New York

Susan Scaggs, Studio Manager, Different Fur Recording, San Francisco, California

Steve Shapiro, Staff Composer, Not Just Jingles, New York, New York

Barbie Springer, Studio Manager, Colorado Sound, Westminster, Colorado

Jim Steinblatt, Communications Manager, ASCAP, New York, New York

Hakim Taylor, Director of Research, RIAA, Washington, D.C.

James Walsh, Studio Manager, Metro Studios. Minneapolis, Minnesota

Thanks also to the following music industry professionals: Kita Bilt, Linda Chancey, Mac Clark, Scott Hiltzik, Greg Klingensmith, John Komara, Don Mack, Cheryl Marshall, Don Menn, Michael Moreale, Jim Peterik, Greg Prestopino, Lisa Vega and Ellen Rose Zucker.

Special thanks to Linda Peterson for her editing expertise.

WHAT'S IN THIS BOOK

Why These Music Careers?   vi

Teddy Riley on How to Find Success
in the Music Business

Famous Beginnings   xiii

Musician/Singer   xiv

Composer/Songwriter   18

Recording Engineer   36

Musical Equipment Salesperson   54

Audio Maintenance Technician   70

Where to Go from Here—School Information   88

Useful Publications   90

Will You Fit into the Music Industry?   92

About the Author   98

WHY THESE MUSIC CAREERS?

Many people enter the music business with visions of stardom and no clear sense of how a long-term career might unfold. Many are successful; more are not, and they go on to other careers after a few years. If you hope to make your living by being directly involved in making music or working with industry pros, you should put personal satisfaction before financial reward. If the two come together, you've struck gold.

In this book you'll find five music careers discussed in detail:

❑ Musician/singer

❑ Composer/songwriter

❑ Recording engineer

❑ Musical equipment salesperson

❑ Audio maintenance technician

Each of these professions is vital to the music industry, and not one of them demands any education beyond the high school level. As in most avenues of the music industry, the requirements for success boil down to talent, hard work and a bit of luck.

People who make their living in the music industry tend to be committed to developing their potential; thus many of them have gone to college and beyond. However, you'll find just as many for whom the pursuit of excellence simply leads from one project to the next, a "school" of experiences that add up to a high degree of professionalism and artistic skill.

Musicians and singers, composers and songwriters, and recording engineers form the creative teams that, under the guidance of producers, make much of the music you hear every day. Musical instrument salespeople keep these cretive people supplied with the means to exercise their talents and express their artistry. And audio maintenance technicians service the high-tech musical instruments and recording equipment that have become essential to contemporary music.

As crucial as these professionals are to the music business, their careers rarely follow a well-defined path. Indeed, the music industry is more like traveling in an untamed jungle: It's difficult to move forward in a straight line and easy to become lost. It's fiercely competitive and driven not by artistic merit, but by bottom-line profits. If you want to be involved, be prepared to sacrifice a regular schedule and a steady paycheck. For those with talent and determination, however, the rewards are great.

TEDDY RILEY

on How to Find Success in the Music Industry

Even in the fast-track business of making hit records, few artists achieve in a lifetime what Teddy Riley has achieved in just a few short years. Bursting onto the scene in 1987 as a member of the R&B trio Guy, Riley—then only 21—wrote and performed on such hits as "Groove Me" and "D-O-G Me Out." As a producer he is responsible for a string of smashes beginning with "I Want

Her" by Keith Sweat (1987) and culminating in Michael Jackson's latest triumph, "Dangerous" (1992). Today the musician whom *USA Today* dubbed a "wunderkind" presides over his own record label, NJS Future Records, dedicated to discovering and introducing the next generation of superstars. His plush recording and production complex, The Future Enterprises, is located in Virginia Beach, Virginia.

Riley's personal trademark is the lean, mean, tightly knit groove known as the "new jack swing." He introduced the sound on Guy's debut album which sold 2 million copies. A variety of influences absorbed during his youth in New York—gospel, funk, pop, R&B and hip-hop—it's the secret ingredient in Riley productions for such stars as Bobby Brown, Jane Child, Al B. Sure!, Soul II Soul, Kool Moe Dee, Salt-n-Pepa, even the legendary Stevie Wonder. His latest work is a new album by Bobby Brown that features a duet with Whitney Houston.

Even after indisputable success in virtually every area of the music industry, Riley, 25, is, as he puts it, "still hungry." Surveying his achievements, one suspects that his is a hunger that can't be satisfied—the hunger of an artist seeking new challenges and modes of expression. Speaking in a quiet voice that belies the gut-level power of his records, Riley talks about the music industry and his place in it and about the prospects for aspiring music industry professionals of the future.

The music industry is different from most others because it's about having fun. In most other careers you can't really extend yourself unless something new comes along. But when you're involved in making music, you're coming up with different musical ideas or new lyrics. You can say, "Hey, this is something new that I came up with." Being a songwriter, a performer, an engineer or a producer is like being a scientist—you're coming up with new formulas. You're researching the future of music.

The most important thing for the future of music is new ideas. There are lots of new high-tech instruments—synthesizers, drum machines, things like that—but good ideas are what make the music that people will still want to listen to years from now. I use the new technology to help me get my work done faster, but real instruments and live bands are going to continue to be important.

Of course, music will change—but you can't say what the differences are going to be. You can only determine that afterward, when people hear it and appreciate it. I didn't start out calling my music the "new jack swing." I only called it that after the hits were made, and I realized that there was no name for the music that I was making.

One thing about the music industry that I hope will change is the politics. There are lots of artists out there who don't know anything about the music business—they only know that they want to be stars. Unfortunately, most of the time it's not *what* you know but *who* you know that matters. Record companies aren't really listening to demo tapes these days, and it can be hard to make the right connections. I was lucky enough to find a manager who could get me in the door. Once I was on the inside, people recognized what I could do. If you have talent, sometimes that's all it takes. But if you're on the outside, it can be very tough to get the recognition you deserve.

I'm trying to change that with my own record company. We listen to all of the tapes that come in. I want to encourage people who are involved in music to keep going because music is a very positive force in people's lives. If they're not involved in music, they might be involved in other things that aren't so positive, like drugs or violence.

Music has always been the most important thing in my life. I played in school bands in elementary school, junior high school and high school. I even played drums in parades when I was in Cub Scouts. Those experiences, plus gigging and jamming on the side, gave me a big head start as a professional.

My first real job was playing keyboards with a band in a nightclub called Jock's Place in Harlem. We performed four nights a week, from 9 at night until 2 in the morning. I made around $600 a week. A lot of people from the industry would go to that club to check out new bands, and that's how I got noticed. Next, I joined a group called Kids At Work. We put out a record; it didn't go very far, but it was a start. Then I got into producing, first rap records and later R&B. I started producing people like Keith Sweat, Bobby Brown, Johnny Kemp, the Jacksons—major artists—

and I was making records and producing with my own band, Guy. That's when things really took off.

Since I always planned to be involved in music, I didn't go to college. But I can't say that I'm not planning to go—it's just that I don't really have the time right now. I have two daughters, and I want them both to go to college. In fact, I'm saving my money so that they can have that experience. So I wouldn't tell anyone not to go. But there are plenty of opportunities in the music industry for people who don't have a four-year degree. In fact, I've seen people in executive positions who never went to college! The chance of making it big is always small, but it doesn't have anything to do with how far you went in school.

It really depends on what you want to do. If you want to be a songwriter, you have to write classic songs. You only get a few chances in this business—you either slam it or jam it. Not that every song that I write is a hit. I'm grateful when people appreciate what I do, but if one person—just one—doesn't like one of my songs, I'll change it. That's because I know there could be a lot of other people who think the way that person does.

If you want to play an instrument, you have to develop the chops to be able to do anything you want to do. Don't worry about competition from machines; like the song says, "Ain't nothing like the real thing." I'm using real musicians in my productions, and I'll be using them when I go on tour with my new band, Blackstreet.

Recording engineers also make a big contribution to my sound. The ones I work with are with me through thick and thin. I'm a perfectionist when it comes to drum sounds: I like my kick drums fat and my snare drums slapping, and that's what they give me. When the mixing board goes down or my speakers blow, I count on the studio technician to fix everything.

And I depend on music stores and salespeople to make sure I get the newest equipment before everyone else does. They should be in contact with the manufacturers so that they can give me what I need up front, so I don't have to come back later and spend even more money.

Right now my biggest challenge is my record company, NJS Future Records. To me this is real life in the music industry. I didn't know it was going to be this hard, but

I'm struggling through it. MCA Records, which is distributing my label, has been like a family to me; they've been very helpful, and I'm learning a lot. It's not like producing records. You have to stay with it every day. It takes all of my attention. It's even keeping me off of the road with Guy. But I'm determined to make the groups who record for me into stars. I want them to be legends.

I never say to myself "I've made it. I'm at the top now." I'm still struggling. That's the only way that I'm going to keep the things I have. When you finally make it, or when you make some money, you can't say, "I've got it now; I don't have to do this any more." You have to be humble. Don't slack up. Keep working. Stay hungry. That's the only way to achieve greatness.

FAMOUS BEGINNINGS

Rock singer/song writer Sinead O'Connor. Her first album, *The Lion and the Cobra*, (1987) went platinum.

Once out of the reformatory where she spent time in her teens for involvement in petty crime, O'Connor's first job was delivering singing telegrams in a French maid's costume.

Rapper Hammer. His single "U Can't Touch This" was Number One simultaneously in *Billboard*'s Pop and Black Singles charts.

Hammer started as the official bat boy for the Oakland A's at age 11 and was promoted to administrative assistant to the team's owner in his teens.

Country/pop singer Garth Brooks. His first album was the first country record to reach Number One in *Billboard*'s Pop chart.

Early in his career Garth worked as a bouncer in a nightclub and later did a stint as a salesperson in a Nashville boot store to supplement his income as a performer.

You hear their work everywhere: on radio and television, in movies and plays, in restaurants, at baseball games, during religious services, even while you're waiting on the phone. "They" are professional musicians and singers, bringing the power of music into your life.

Yet for most, establishing a career is an elusive goal. Opportunities to play for money are few, and the number of hopefuls is enormous. They are willing to forego the security of a regular job for a shot at the big time or simply for the satisfaction of performing. They spend endless hours rehearsing for what may amount to only a short time on stage.

There are many niches for musicians and singers, depending on their goals and talents, and how hard they're willing to fight for success. Rock and country bands that play current hits can find steady work at bars, weddings, hotel lounges and on cruise ships. Or players can freelance in temporary pick-up bands at nightclubs, parties and theatrical performances. Those who don't enjoy performing for an audience can record music for commercials, records or television scores. Those who insist on playing their own music in their own way, of course, travel the hardest road.

Singers and instrumentalists don't climb any particular ladder—they simply get out there and work. They do small-scale gigs at first, then larger ones as they gain experience, confidence and recognition. The best preparation is to be as comfortable as possible with yourself as a musician, whether that means practicing your instrument behind closed doors or jumping on stage immediately. Even if you're not among the lucky few who reach the top of the field, you will always have the satisfaction of having developed your own talent.

◆ **Getting into the Field**

What You Need to Know

❏ Technological aspects of your instrument (how it works, how to keep it in good repair and make the instrument sound its best)
❏ Characteristics of various musical styles
❏ Harmony (the construction and uses of various chords)
❏ Arrangement and/or orchestration (the distribution of notes among various instruments; helpful to know if you are asked to play without a predetermined arrangement)
❏ Music theory and history (helpful for interpreting and conceptualizing music)
❏ The audio recording process (if you play on recordings)

Necessary Skills

❏ Play an instrument and/or sing
❏ A natural sense of rhythm, pitch and musical style
❏ Ability to arrange, or make up an appropriate instrumental part, for your instrument (necessary in many situations)
❏ Read music (necessary in some situations)
❏ Ability to produce a "demo," or demonstration recording, of your work (necessary in many situations)

Do You Have What It Takes?

❏ Self-motivation and persistence
❏ Discipline to put in long hours
❏ Patience (people may ask you to play the same songs over and over; you may have wait your turn to perform)
❏ High self-esteem (you need to believe in yourself even when you don't get the response you hope for)
❏ Outgoing personality, verging on show-off
❏ Ability to work as part of a team (each person, even a solo performer, has his or her own role, which con-

tributes to the final sound)
❏ Ability to do your job and remain upbeat under stress
❏ Ability to ''think on your feet'' (you may have to ad lib before an audience or act like you know what you're doing when you are unprepared)
❏ Artistic vision (ability to imagine the sound you want and communicate it to others)
❏ Diplomacy (ability to deal with difficult people)
❏ Punctuality (showing up on time is essential)

Education

No formal education is required, although most musicians and singers take lessons to improve their technique. Training in instrumental/vocal performance skills is recommended, as is training in ensemble performance (playing as part of a group).

Training in all academic subject areas of music (music theory, music history, orchestration, arrangement, harmony, counterpoint, composition, etc.) is recommended for interpreting music, communicating with other musicians and understanding the musical requirements of a given project.

Licenses Required

None. For instrumentalists, membership in the American Federation of Musicians (AF of M) is necessary for some kinds of work. For singers, membership in the Screen Actors Guild (SAG) or the American Federation of Television and Radio Announcers (AFTRA) may be necessary for television or radio commercials and record albums.

Job Outlook

Competition for jobs: very competitive
There is always some demand for musicians. However, the number of nightclubs, bars and private parties that feature live music has greatly decreased with the recession of the early nineties. Even on Broadway, instrumental ensembles are being replaced by recordings or electronic instru-

ments. When fewer commercials are being made, both instrumentalists and vocalists are affected, and synthesizers have usurped the roles of many traditional instruments as well. What's more, while record companies are signing many new bands, their overall release schedules are being pared down.

Bleak prospects aside, the world of music is diverse enough that there are always opportunities of one kind or another. With an objective sense of your own talent, reasonable goals, thick skin, unshakable commitment and a dollop of luck, you're likely to be able to find a niche—or invent one of your own.

◆ **The Ground Floor**

There is no official way to get into playing or singing for a living. Generally, a career begins by performing before an audience. For hopeful rock, jazz and folk players, opportunities include evening gigs at local bars, coffee houses, nightclubs, dances, parties and the like. Theaters and churches offer a chance to perform as well. Some management companies put together touring bands that play Top 40 hits at hotels and on cruise ships, which can get a musician's career off to a solid start. Singers can attract a following by playing at open-mike night events at bars and clubs. Bands can organize their own concerts, or showcases, for specially invited club owners or record company contacts.

Recording a demo tape to play for club owners and record company people is a helpful entry-level move. Some inexperienced performers play on demonstration recordings (demos) for other entertainers and songwriters. Low-budget films, commercials and records offer some entry-level recording opportunities.

◆ **On-the-Job Responsibilities**

Beginners and Experienced Musicians
❏ Practice in preparation for performance
❏ Schedule rehearsals and performances
❏ Show up on time
❏ Bring a working instrument

❑ Perform to the employer's satisfaction
❑ Come up with your own parts (what you play or sing) if necessary
❑ Transport equipment

Established players have managers and agents to book their sessions or appearances and can afford to hire roadies and cartage companies to haul their gear from job to job.

When You'll Work

Singers and musicians never work regular hours. Stage performers tend to work in the evenings (late night hours are the norm for rock and jazz musicians) and, of course, on weekends. Recording musicians and singers may work at any hour. Commercials and film scores tend to be recorded during weekday business hours; music is recorded first, vocals afterward, so singers usually have to work in the afternoon. Sessions for records are more likely to begin at night, any day of the week, and may last until dawn.

Time Off

Holidays are usually the busiest times for performers who work in nightclubs and bars. Those who record for the advertising or film industries are less likely to work on major holidays. Since a musician's or singer's business is generally freelance, you may find yourself with a lot of days off it you're not successful. Those who have a good reputation and are in demand can usually schedule days off as they prefer.

Busy seasons vary from year to year. Those who play "casuals," or weddings and other kinds of parties, find themselves most busy in the summer and during the winter holidays. Within the record industry there is usually a lull during late winter and late summer.

Perks

❑ Publicity—local, regional, national and even international
❑ Possibility of "special thanks" or other credit on compact discs
❑ Merchandise discounts (offered by some stores to

professionals, and offered by manufacturers in return for endorsements)
❑ Free admission to concerts (sometimes)

❑ Bars, coffee houses, nightclubs, dance halls, restaurants, hotels, amusement parks, etc.
❑ Individual musicians and musical groups
❑ Composers and songwriters
❑ Music production companies (which put together music for records, advertising, film and/or television)
❑ Management companies (who hire musicians to accompany their artists on tours)
❑ Talent agencies (who book performers for parties and similar events)
❑ Record companies
❑ Theaters and theater companies
❑ Private individuals for weddings, parties and other special events
❑ Contractors (who hire musicians for recordings)

◆ **Who's Hiring**

Beginning and experienced musicians: potential for a lot of travel.

◆ **Places You'll Go**

Touring with midtier groups such as nostalgia acts offers young performers good experience, and top touring musicians are paid quite well. This kind of travel, however, is notoriously grueling. Some performers enjoy it, but just as many find it one of the less pleasant aspects of their profession. International festivals of folk, bluegrass, jazz and other styles of music offer more comfortable travel opportunities. Beginners who want to tour can connect with an agent who books bands for national hotel chains or cruise ships.

Musicians and singers who record commercials and film scores tend to stay in one place as do those who play in pick-up bands for weddings and other "casual dates." Rock, jazz and country bands often find it advantageous to build up a following in one area rather than be on tour continually.

Surroundings

The concert stage is the workplace for live performers. Even in a nightclub, where decor may be down-and-dirty, the stage is a special place to be. However, backstage dressing rooms in most performance facilities are usually cramped and undecorated. Rented rehearsal spaces aren't any more cheerful. Touring musicians spend much of their offstage time cooped up in a truck or bus, or in a cheap hotel room waiting for the performance.

Recording musicians and singers can expect to spend quite a bit of time waiting in a record studio lobby. These range from cramped and dull to quite lavish.

Dollars And Cents

Job opportunities for singers and musicians are so diverse that earning potential varies greatly. Steady, modestly good-paying situations do exist, but the work often seems to boil down to the old adage, feast or famine.

Up-and-coming singer/songwriters and bands can expect to play for free, or close to it, much of the time. Aspiring session players and singers may have to play for free in order to make contacts and develop a demo tape. Inexperienced touring players must make do with low wages. Even well-established performers may have a hard time making ends meet. The union-approved hourly wage for session players looks quite generous ($78 to $234 per hour), but it's nearly impossible to fill a 40-hour week doing such work.

Film, television, commercials and Broadway shows usually pay well. Musicians who sign a contract with a major label usually receive a large lump sum, but they may not get another cent if their records don't sell. However, singers and musicians may make a small amount of money in "residuals" every time a recorded performance is broadcast on television and radio, which can add up.

Of course, at the top of the business, the pay scales are extraordinarily high. Pop megastars are among the richest people in the world, and even a successful jingle singer can make a seven-figure income.

There's no formula for success as a musician or singer. Still, if no one knows who you are, no degree of talent will help, so most professional musicians go out of their way to cultivate contacts. A good sense of humor and generally pleasant personality count for a lot when you're working with a group and can give you the edge over performers of equal skill.

Generally, rock and roll bands and singer/songwriters who develop a regional audience and put out a few self-produced records may eventually attract the attention of a record company that markets their talent to a wider audience. Session players and singers may develop a demo tape by playing for free on recording sessions and then send the tape out to potential employers. Eventually, relationships and word-of-mouth recommendations develop into steady work.

Entrepreneurial skills come in handy, especially for those who hope to organize and promote a band. Owning good instruments, appropriate attire, transportation and rehearsal space can make a big difference. In addition, it's important to keep up with new styles and sounds and stay on top of new technological developments.

◆ **Moving Up**

Los Angeles, New York, Chicago and Nashville offer the most opportunities and have both the highest and the lowest pay scales. Minneapolis, San Francisco, Austin, Dallas and Atlanta form the second tier.

Jobs are less plentiful outside of the major centers, but every area offers some work; even the smallest town has church services and private parties.

◆ **Where the Jobs Are**

For singers, both male and female voices are equally in demand. Among instrumentalists, men far outnumber women. Although it may matter whether you're male or female for the purposes of a performing group's image, in most cases, success as a performer is based on merit.

The worlds of rock, jazz, rap and other popular styles

◆ **The Male/Female Equation**

are mostly male. However, more women than ever are playing the instruments used in those styles.

Making Your Decision: What to Consider

The Bad News

❏ The music business is often more business than music
❏ Your work is often judged by people who have little or no musical background
❏ Unpredictable hours and income
❏ No job security (virtually all work is freelance)
❏ Rejection is common
❏ Working under time pressure (in studios)

The Good News

❏ Fulfillment through artistic expression
❏ Creative work; no job is ever the same
❏ Avoidance of structured nine-to-five employment
❏ Informal dress and manners on the job
❏ Opportunity to be the center of attention (on stage)
❏ Possibility (however small) of fame and fortune

More Information Please

American Federation of Musicians
1501 Broadway, Suite 600
New York, New York 10036
800-762-3444
212-869-1330

Write for free pamphlets on touring, recording and other aspects of playing music for a living. Local chapters offer various services to members.

Recording Musicians of America
5711 Klump Avenue
North Hollywood, California 91601
818-364-1899

The organization publishes a directory of member musicians listed by instrument and a summary of union scale rates for recording musicians.

Glenn Phillips, 42,
recording artist,
Atlanta, Georgia
Years in the business: 25

How did you break into performing music for a living?
When I picked up a guitar for the first time, my mind was
filled with sounds. I said, "This is what I'm going to do
for the rest of my life." In high school I started the Hampton Grease Band with some friends, and we started playing
for 50¢ apiece at a seedy little blues club on the wrong side
of town.

Was that a usual way to start?
Probably not now. Music has become bigger business, and
a lot of young bands that I talk to seem to be dealing with
cut-throat businessmen. When we were playing for 50¢, it
wasn't the most rewarding experience financially, but it
wasn't humiliating. It was enriching. A lot of young bands
now are finding that they have to deal with club owners in
a way that's actually humiliating.

11

What experiences prepared you for a career as a musician?

I didn't take formal lessons, but I played with another guitarist who could really play, which was a big influence. I went to the library to study books on music theory. Also, I traded guitar lessons for piano lessons and rock guitar lessons for classical lessons. I acquired a lot of knowledge.

How many different bands have you been in?

For the first six years of my career, the Hampton Grease Band was my main focus. We put out our first album on Columbia. Since that band broke up, I've put out nine solo albums and played on a few other peoples' albums. You know, ever since I started doing this, people from record companies have said, "I love the records, but you've got to make them more marketable." My intention has always been to create music that was timeless, so it's the artistic pursuit that sustains me. I've now been making records for 15 years, and most of those record company guys don't have jobs anymore. I'm not gloating; I'm just saying that you have to determine your own priorities if you're going to get into this.

What do you do in a day's work?

I spend part of the day going through tape, or on the phone. Band rehearsals are usually between 6:30 and 11:00 at night. Then I work on tapes until about 6 A.M. I'm always in the process of recording something. I live in a duplex; we live in one half, and the other half is my studio. I work out all of the ideas there. I can't afford to do it in a real studio.

The band is touring less than ever before because so many clubs have closed. We used to tour up and down the East Coast for six weeks at a time—now it's more like playing on weekends.

What do you like most about your work?

The connection with people I've played with has been most meaningful. You pursue it as a process of creating music, but on special occasions it transcends that, and you have incredible experiences with people that you wouldn't have any other way.

What do you like least?

Dealing with business. In order to keep your music alive, you have to be incredibly personally involved and committed. But in order to deal with the business end of it, you have to flip a switch and not take anything personally; you have to learn to laugh at the insults. You know, the people who care most about music get weeded out first.

What advice would you offer someone who's considering a career as a musician?

A lot of people ask me, "Should I get involved in music as a career?" My answer has always been, "If you have to think about it, you probably shouldn't." Unless it's such a compulsion that you have no choice but to pursue it as your life's work, you're really better off keeping it as something you can enjoy part time. Otherwise, the business end of it will either corrupt you or defeat you.

If you do have that compulsion, then you have to realize that you can't count on bringing in money consistently. You're going to have to find a way to survive rough economic times.

Emily Bindiger, 37,
freelance studio singer,
New York, New York
Years in the business: 22; 9 as a studio singer

How did you break into singing for a living?

It was a roundabout kind of thing. I have a background in theater, singing and acting in Broadway shows, TV shows and movies. I was doing a children's TV show and there was a lot of music involved. It was recorded at a jingle recording studio, and they saw that I was capable of doing that kind of work. My first jobs were for the same people who had written the music for the children's show. As the show wound down, I got more and more studio work, enough to put a tape together to send to other producers.

What experiences prepared you for your career?

I was always studying music and singing as a kid, but I

really wanted to be an actress. I went to the High School for Performing Arts in New York as a drama major. I was very sure that I wanted to do something in the performing arts. When it looked like I was going to be doing studio work, I decided to brush up on music theory, harmony, sight-reading and stuff like that, even though it wasn't necessary.

What was the hardest aspect of working in this field during your first few years?
Being intimidated by other people who had been around longer than I had. I had to overcome that. I had to tell myself, "There's a reason I'm here. They like my voice. I belong here," and just hang in. I still feel that way sometimes.

How long did it take you to get established?
About five years. There were people who hired me over and over again, so I would be established with one particular producer, but nobody else. By now, most producers in New York know who I am.

What do you do in a day's work?
Normally, vocal sessions take place in the afternoon because they spend the morning recording the musical tracks. I come in, find out what the style of the spot is, the content and what it's for, and then I sing it. Usually you learn it as you go, and the producer tells you what he wants. You just do it until they like it. Sometimes it takes a minute, sometimes it takes hours. I'll do between one and four of those in a day, either as a soloist or singing in a background group.

What do you like most about your work?
A lot of things. The fact that it's not a nine-to-five job. I can pick my own vacation days. When you're doing commercials you have most of your weekends free. And the camaraderie—everybody's together making music.

What do you like least?
You have to deal with a lot of jerks in this business.

What's your proudest achievement?
Singing for the soundtrack of the movie version of *A Chorus Line*. The final product wasn't the greatest, but while

we were doing it, it was very exciting. The arrangements were incredible and very, very difficult. There were 16 of us in the studio, all reading different parts. The director, Richard Attenborough, would run out into the studio after a really good take and say, "Why argue with perfection?"

What advice would you offer someone thinking about a career as a studio singer?
You have to really love it. There's a lot of competition for very few jobs. There are a lot of talented people who aren't working, and a lot of not-so-talented people who are. If you're still in your teens, you may have to spend a few years doing something else, because commercials don't have much use for people that age. That doesn't mean you have to stop singing. You can sing in clubs, at weddings, on records. Use that time to study music; learn to read it. Go to clubs, listen to the radio, buy records, pay attention to commercials. Have a clear idea of what's going to be expected of you, and be as ready as you can be to do it.

Brad Rabuchin, 36,
freelance musician,
Canoga Park, California
Years in the business: 13

How did you break into playing music for a living?
I've just tried to meet people and convince them I can play well. I'm still breaking in in terms of doing what I really want to do. I'd like to be recording albums with a group, writing my own material, touring.

What was your first paying job?
Playing with a blues-rock band at a pizza parlor near my house. I was one year out of high school. We had played at parties and things like that, and we convinced the manager that it would be cool to have a band. We played there on weekends for about a month or two.

Was that a usual way of getting started?
I think so. You start playing and opportunities present themselves. We were just playing and trying to improve.

What experiences prepared you to be a professional musician?

I had some good guitar teachers. I went to junior college pretty much exclusively for music. While I was there, I hooked up with other players who were up and coming. I played with them a lot, just jamming, and that was the most valuable thing. But most of what I've learned has been just by doing it. I've gone out on a gig really unqualified, crashed and burned, and learned from that.

Taking lessons and going to college helps, but what you come up against in the real world is a very different thing. In terms of the business, I'm still learning how to do that. Whenever I lose a job or don't get a gig, I try to analyze why and fix that. I'm always trying to develop better communication skills, learning how to market myself, figuring out what equipment I need, and all that stuff.

What was the hardest aspect of being a musician during your first few years?

Just realizing how far I had to go. Also, dealing with the times when things weren't going well, when I didn't have any gigs. Whenever that happened I'd do a lot of teaching—at one time I had over 40 students. And when I first started teaching, I wasn't qualified at all. I was thinking, "I'm teaching people and I'm hardly better than they are!"

How long did it take to get established?

It's gone back and forth. There have been times that I've done well for a while, and then the bottom drops out. Recently I played guitar for "The Simpsons" TV show. I got paid really well, but that made me think, "Why don't I get paid that way all the time?" So I'm not really satisfied with my success. But I'm a lot more comfortable than I used to be; I've adjusted my expectations.

How many jobs have you had?

Thousands, literally, if we're talking about all of the parties, clubs, recording situations, groups. It's mostly one-shot gigs. I played on a cruise ship for about four months. For the past four years, I've had a regular gig with a jazz-fusion quartet on Tuesday nights. That's far longer than I've done anything else.

What do you like most about your work?

I like the fact that I'm playing. I still enjoy it, unless the people are weird or it's with bad players. I like the challenge of playing well, and the variety.

What do you like least?

The unreliability. It's cool that every week is different, but that's the bad part, too. There's a lot of financial pressure. It's taken me a long time to get a credit card—I didn't have one until last year. My car isn't that great. There are times when all I have is my Tuesday night gig for a week or two. I seem to always have enough money to get through those times, but it's scary.

What do you do in a day's work?

I spend a lot of time on the phone, scheduling rehearsals and gigs, finding players for gigs that I put together, selling myself, looking for studios for recording projects, that kind of stuff. During the day I might have a recording session and then a gig at night. If I can fit in a little practicing, I'll do that.

What advice would you offer to someone who's interested in playing or singing for a living?

Play with as many people as you can and meet people who arc already doing it. Try to learn from them and try to hook up with them as sources of gigs. Practicing is important, but a lot of it is people knowing about you. You can be the greatest player in the world, but if people aren't aware of your skills, they'll never call you.

COMPOSER/ SONGWRITER

Virtually every event that includes music requires the talents of a composer or a songwriter. Songwriters supply material for untold numbers of recording artists. Ad agencies employ people to create music for TV and radio spots. Composers score (write the music for) TV shows and movies, as well as corporate presentations. Even the bloops and bleeps of video games have to be composed by someone!

The most celebrated of these creative professionals are the hitmakers of Top 40 radio, who often perform their own songs. Some professionals live for years on the income generated by only one or two hit songs. Still, composing and songwriting provide very few people with a steady income. Projects with large budgets are few, and the possibility that any given composition will become a hit are slim. It's not

19

uncommon for people in this field to also work in other areas of the music business or to hold a day job.

Composers who work for a music publisher or a company that produces advertising music (a jingle house) may work in an office. Most others, however, work at home on a freelance basis. In either case, they must be able to produce demonstration recordings (demos) of their work. This usually involves being familiar with high-tech music production equipment such as synthesizers and computers.

If you write music for a rock or jazz band, or make up tunes while practicing your instrument, you're starting in the same place as many of the world's most popular composers and songwriters. To get more exposure, you might consider offering to supply music for performing groups or media production facilities within your area, including local theaters, churches, school radio and student filmmakers.

Who knows? With hard work, persistence and talent, you may pen your own hit song.

What You Need to Know

◆ **Getting into the Field**

❑ Music theory (helpful for conceptualizing music and communicating with other musicians)

❑ Arrangement and/or orchestration (the distribution of notes among various instruments)

❑ Harmony (the construction and uses of various chords)

❑ Characteristic sounds and capabilities of a variety of instruments

❑ Characteristics of various musical styles

❑ Music history (helpful for understanding various musical styles)

❑ The audio recording process

❑ Operation of MIDI (musical instrument digital interface) devices and other computerized music production equipment

❑ The process of television, video and film production (if composing for these media)

Necessary Skills

❑ Originate musical ideas and flesh them out into finished compositions or songs

❑ Play at least one instrument, preferably keyboard and/or guitar

❑ Sing (helpful but not absolutely necessary)

❑ Ability to arrange for a variety of instruments

❑ Read music (necessary in some situations)

❑ Legible handwriting of notes and other musical symbols (necessary in some situations)

❑ Be able to conduct (direct the musicians through the music; helpful but often not necessary)

Do You Have What It Takes?

❑ Ability to work in relative isolation and as part of a team

❑ Patience (coming up with the right melody or words can take time)

❑ Self-motivation and persistence
❑ Punctuality and reliability (showing up on time and meeting deadlines are essential)
❑ Ability to accept and respond constructively to criticism
❑ Diplomacy (ability to deal with difficult people)
❑ Artistic vision (ability to imagine the sound you want and communicate it to others)
❑ Willingness to work long hours

Education

No formal education is necessary. Courses in audio recording are helpful for making demos, and courses in synthesis, computer literacy and MIDI can teach you how to use high-tech music production equipment. Training in all academic subject areas of music (music theory, music history, harmony, counterpoint, orchestration, arranging, composition) helps to make a composer more versatile, and some training in conducting can help ensure good performances of your compositions.

Licenses Required

None

Job Outlook

Competition for jobs: very competitive
The music business used to be a clique of highly trained composers, arrangers, orchestrators, copyists, performers and recording engineers. With the advent of low-cost, easy-to-operate recording equipment and MIDI systems, it has become possible for one person to compose, arrange, perform and record an entire production. To the extent that this reduces the costs of producing music, it results in more work for composers and songwriters. On the other hand, it creates even more competition for the few jobs that pay well.

The recession of the early nineties has made such jobs—particularly those in advertising—less plentiful than ever.

However, the music business in general continues to thrive, and those whose skills and talents match the demands of the market continue to do well.

Entry-Level Work

- ❑ Songwriter for a band
- ❑ Solo singer/songwriter
- ❑ Freelance composer for student films, local theater, church groups, low-budget commercials or public service announcements
- ❑ Assistant at a jingle house or other music production company

If you have no credits but can supply a tape of your work, you might get started by sending it to music production companies, song publishers, music libraries and any other possible source of paid work. Songwriters may be "discovered" while performing their own material in nightclubs. If you're in a band that meets with local success, you may be able to capitalize on it by selling your songs to performers with a broader audience.

The few entry-level positions that exist for composers and songwriters are very specialized. In the world of film and television scoring, aspiring composers can start as orchestrators and copyists. In advertising the most direct route is to land a job as an assistant at a jingle house.

Beginners

Music production company assistants help composers, producers and office staff in any way required, whether it's tidying the office, doing paperwork or making coffee. There also may be some basic musical duties.

Experienced Composers/Songwriters

- ❑ Meet with the client to determine the style, budget, timetable, medium and other aspects of the project
- ❑ Compose appropriate music

❑ Write lyrics or hire a lyricist (if necessary)

❑ Arrange or orchestrate the music, or hire an arranger or orchestrator

❑ Hire musicians (if no contractor or producer is involved)

❑ Conduct the ensemble or hire a conductor

❑ Schedule and supervise recording sessions (if no producer is involved)

Songwriters under contract to a music publisher must deliver a yearly quota of songs, subject to approval by the publisher.

When You'll Work

Music publishers, production houses and other companies that have a staff of composers and/or songwriters may offer a relatively regular schedule.

Because music is often the last element to be added to a film, video or theatrical production, when things are running behind schedule, the composer is usually on a very tight deadline. This may mean working around the clock for days (in commercials) or weeks (in film and television) in order to meet the production schedule. In contrast, songwriters who supply popular recording groups, school bands and other clients without sharply defined deadlines can write when they prefer and sell their songs later.

Time Off

Vacation is a luxury among busy composers and songwriters. When work is steady, it's impractical to take time off. When things are slow, spare time can be put to use hustling up business. Freelancers determine their own schedule, although they risk losing clients if they're on vacation. The slow seasons are usually late summer, before the record, film and advertising industries gear up for the holiday season, and late winter, after the holiday production schedule is finished. Major holidays are usually free.

Perks

❑ Potential for the free services of musicians for personal recording projects

❑ Free or discount-priced access to studio equipment

during unbooked hours
- ❑ Free admission to concerts on occasion
- ❑ Composition or songwriter credit on compact disc covers, film credits, program notes, etc.

- ❑ Jingle houses (production companies specializing in music for commercials)
- ❑ Television, film and/or video production companies
- ❑ Theater groups
- ❑ Music publishing companies
- ❑ Record producers
- ❑ Recording artists who don't compose their own material

◆ **Who's Hiring**

Beginners and experienced professionals: slight potential for travel.

If you aren't based in a major city, you may travel to other cities in the U.S. to meet with clients and to take advantage of talent and services available in a more central location.

◆ **Places You'll Go**

A composer works either at a desk with pencil, paper and a musical instrument, or at the helm of a high-tech music workstation. In either case, the necessary equipment can fit into a small corner, cubicle or office. It's likely that you'll do most of your composing in your own home. Should one of your pieces be recorded, you'll spend a day or two in a recording studio, which may be bustling or subdued. Modern recording studios range from stylish to thoroughly trashed out, but in virtually all cases they consist of one or two small rooms crammed with equipment.

◆ **Surroundings**

As in any creative field, income varies enormously. Hit songs, major film scores, weekly television series and high-profile commercials can make their creators rich. On the other hand, a songwriter may write any number of songs without selling one, and a jingle composer may submit any number of demos without having one selected for final

◆ **Dollars and Cents**

25

production. The budget paid to a composer of a film score may only cover the costs of musician and recording, but composers often do it for the experience and credit.

Most composers and songwriters sell their work (or some share in it, or some right to use it) for a flat fee called a creative fee, advance or draw. Later they may collect royalties depending on how often their composition is performed and/or broadcast. Fees vary tremendously. If there's a third party involved (such as a production company), the composer may retain only a small percentage of any fees and/or royalty income. Jingle composers often make up for this by singing in the background chorus, which makes them eligible for pay under the generous union contracts for vocalists.

Moving Up ◆ Until you've established a reputation, your stature as a professional will be judged by the quality of the compositions on your demo tape. If you hope to work in film, television or television commercials, you'll need to show a videotape of productions that you have scored. If you can land a few jobs with famous names, that alone may be enough to guarantee your future for at least a while. Eventually a successful track record with some well-known names will establish your professionalism and reliability.

In the meantime, you must keep abreast of new musical styles and sounds and be able to recreate them on demand. It's also important to develop a network of musicians who can perform your compositions with flair.

Where the Jobs Are ◆ For composers and songwriters the centers of business are Los Angeles (for records as well as film and television scores), New York (records, commercials and musical theater), Chicago (commercials) and Nashville (records, particularly country music). Elsewhere, jobs are less plentiful and tend to involve local advertising. Minneapolis, San Francisco, Dallas and Atlanta offer some opportunities.

Female songwriters have played a prominent role in rock, jazz and other popular music since the early sixties, although the most successful tend to be performers as well. Behind the scenes the lion's share of songwriting and composing is done by men. There's no particular barrier to women, however, and a number have made it to the top of the field, particularly writing music for commercials.

◆ **The Male/Female Equation**

The Bad News
❏ Demanding clients who may expect countless revisions
❏ Having your work judged on grounds that aren't strictly musical
❏ Having to be creative on demand
❏ Long, unpredictable work hours
❏ Unsteady, often low, income
❏ No job security or standard benefits (almost all work is freelance)

The Good News
❏ Excitement of hearing your work on the air
❏ Opportunity to be involved in making music
❏ Not having to work nine to five every day
❏ Working with state-of-the-art music technology
❏ Possibility of working with famous musicians
❏ Possibility—however small—of fame and fortune

◆ **Making Your Decision: What to Consider**

American Society of Composers, Authors and Publishers (ASCAP)
One Lincoln Plaza
New York, New York 10035
212-682-7227

For nonmembers, the organization sponsors songwriter workshops and showcases around the country in all musical categories. It also provides competitions and scholarships. There's also a monthly meeting open to nonmembers.

◆ **More Information Please**

Broadcast Music Inc. (BMI)
320 West 57th Street
New York, New York 10019
212-586-2000

You can get brochures describing opportunities and the technicalities of composing for money by writing this organization, which collects performance rights license fees for member songwriters and composers. It also offers free composing workshops in various styles for members.

Nashville Songwriters Association International (NSAI)
803 18th Avenue South
Nashville, Tennessee 37203
615-321-5004

This organization offers free song evaluation service by mail for members. They also have weekly songwriting workshops in various cities around the country for members.

WHAT IT'S REALLY LIKE

Billy Yates, 28,
staff songwriter,
HoriPro Entertainment
Group, Inc.,
Nashville, Tennessee
Years in the business: Ten in music;
one in songwriting

What is your musical background?
My family did a radio show in Missouri, where I grew up,
so I was around music as long as I can remember. I did a
lot of singing in churches. When I was 13 and my voice
started changing, I was shy about it and I quit singing alto-
gether. When I got out of high school, I auditioned at a
theater where they had a country music show, and I got on
the show. I stayed with that for about three years. Then I
made a vacation trip to Nashville, and it really caught my
attention. I got up my courage and moved here.

How did you break into writing songs?
I was trying to get something happening as a singer, doing
showcases, which is where you book a club and you invite
industry people to see you. At one of the showcases, a pro-

ducer named Ray Baker came up to me and said, "If you don't hear from any of the record labels, I'd like to talk to you." He put me in contact with the publishing company I'm working for now, HoriPro.

They pay me a draw every week. When royalties start coming in on the songs that I write, they'll start recouping the money they've given me. I'll start earning royalties once they've recouped the entire draw. My quota is 10 songs per year. Anything I write over that applies to the next year. I've written 30 songs so far this year, so I'm caught up for three years. If they like them, they'll make demo recordings and pitch the songs to record labels and artists.

Was that a usual way to start?
I think so, although I wasn't going after a songwriting contract as aggressively as most people.

What's the hardest aspect of working in this field?
The rejection—you turn songs in, and maybe nobody gets excited. It's especially difficult if it's something you really believe in, that you're really proud of, and somebody shoots it down. But you have to take that in stride. No one person knows what's going to make it—you have to remember that.

What do you do in a day's work?
Today I started writing at 9 A.M. with one guy and wrote until 1 P.M. Then I had another writing appointment from 2 P.M. until 6 P.M. In the evening sometimes I do songwriters' nights, where I go on stage at a smaller club with my guitar. And I still do stuff with a band every once in a while.

What do you like most about your work as a songwriter?
I love the challenge of finding a great idea and then following through with it. And of course, the payoff can be great. Once you sign a songwriting deal, there's automatically more respect. Everybody knows how hard that is, and everyone treats you a little differently. That's a big reward.

What do you like least?
Just about every writer goes through dry spells when you don't seem to have any ideas. There are weeks when I just don't think of anything, and I start to wonder, "Is it over?"

What is your proudest achievement?

Well, I recently got my first cut, and it was by George Jones. They're saying it'll be the single and the title cut of the album, although you never can be sure until it happens. Then, after that deal came through, they pitched another one of my songs to George, and he just recorded it. That's a real good feeling.

What advice would you give to someone who's interested in being a songwriter?

Be really objective about your own abilities. Sometimes you've got to fake confidence; you have to at least appear to believe in yourself to get anything done. But you also have to be able to stand back and look at your work and say, "Is this really good, or is it bad?" Don't always listen to what your closest friends say. A lot of people will give you false hope. But if you really do believe in it and you're determined to do it, don't give up.

Rod McBrien, 48,
composer/producer, president,
Rod McBrien Productions,
New York, New York
Years in the business: 30

What's your musical background?

I've always loved music. The first instrument I played was drums, then I picked up guitar because I wanted to be a little more musical. In high school I had bands, wrote songs, made records—I even had a local hit record in New York. And of course, I did weddings and bar mitzvahs—I paid my dues. And I could always write songs.

How did you break into writing music for a living?

I was fascinated by recording studios, and I got my first full-time job as an engineer. I engineered "Leader of the Pack," by the Shang-Ri-La's. Later I did a lot of freelancing and worked with great musicians like Jimi Hendrix, the Grateful Dead, Neil Diamond. All that time I wrote songs. I always had a studio available to me, so I produced stuff for various record labels and put out a few records on RCA with another guy under the name Stark & McBrien. We made some pretty good records, but nothing big happened.

A jazz musician named Don Elliot was pretty famous in those days, and he had a music house that did lots of big commercials. His wife ran it, and my wife knew her. One time when a job came in, his wife called me and said, "Why don't you take a shot at it?" So I got started doing commercials with Don Elliot Productions, and we got hot!

Was that a usual way to get started?

I don't know what the usual way is. You've got to be there, bang on doors, meet people, network, whatever. Luck has a lot to do with it. The best gig I ever had was an association with the McCann-Erickson advertising agency. I was on an airplane going to Nashville, and it turned out that my seatmate was the music director at McCann-Erickson. I had worked for him before, and we respected each other. He said, "You know, I really believe in fate. I think you should come to work for me." Just from sitting next to him on the plane! I got a weekly retainer to write for them.

When did you finally feel established?

When I won the American Song Festival, the first year they had it. That was nice—the prize was $30,000. I was in my late twenties. My parents always used to say, "When are you going to get a job?" But when I won that contest and got that exposure and all that money, suddenly I was a songwriter. It was thrilling.

What other jobs have you held?

I had a staff songwriting job at one point with Mercury Records' publishing company. I also had a deal with Metromedia Music; I'd get an automatic advance on every song I gave them. Eventually I was director of A&R (artists and repertoire) for their label, which was short lived.

What do you do in a day's work?

Once I get an assignment, I start writing, or call in other writers if I need help, and put a presentation together. Then I stay on top of it, because there are always other people trying to get the same job. I write the song, put together the best demo I can and keep my fingers crossed.

What do you like most about your work?
I love being creative and hearing my stuff on the air. That part is a lot of fun.

What do you like least?
The selling. It's always a hustle, and you have to make everything happen by yourself. If you've got a song, you have to bang on doors to get somebody to record it or get some record company to give you a production deal so you can pick up a few bucks and stay in the game.

What's your proudest achievement?
I've scored the Orange Bowl football half-time show for the last few years; I'm proud of that. I put a lot into it. I wrote the finale song for it this year, and I think I made a statement with it. I'm proud of commercials, too, but it's a different kind of thing.

What advice would you offer to someone who's interested in a career as a songwriter or composer?
Well, they say that if there's nothing else you really can do or want to do, then you have to go for it. But if there's something else you'd be happy doing, you should do that instead. This is a tough racket. There's just not an awful lot of work out there, and there are more and more people trying to break in.

Patterson Barrett, 38,
composer, co-president of
Barrett & Harwell Music,
Austin, Texas
Years in the business: ten

What's your musical background?
As a kid I played trumpet and trombone in grade school. We had a piano in the house, which I taught myself to play; same thing with the guitar. During high school I switched from public school to a progressive private school. There, I took several music courses: composition, sight singing, ear training and so forth. I joined a band during the summer right after high school and we all went to live on a farm in upstate New York. While I was there, I played on a Jerry

33

Jeff Walker record. After that, the band moved to California. When I left the band, I moved to Austin because I'd met a lot of musicians who said it was a great place to be.

How did you break into writing music?
My current partner was an engineer at a studio that did a lot of advertising work. He knew me from playing in bars and clubs. One day he called me to do some very simple music tracks. He'd say, "We need a 30-second guitar track that will go along with this," or "We need a 60-second piano track that goes with this," and I'd write it on the spot. After we did that for about a year, we decided to call ourselves a company.

Is that the usual way to get started?
I'm sure a lot of people start small, like I did, and then get hired on at a larger production company. You start from the ground up.

How long did it take you to get established?
After we became a business officially, it didn't take long. There weren't a lot of composers and producers in Austin conducting themselves as businesses. Plus my partner had day-to-day contact with people in the advertising industry. We send out demo reels to get new business, but mostly people come to us.

What do you do in a typical day?
I make about a third of my income composing commercials, a third from performing and another third from engineering other people's projects. I do almost everything at one studio, which is also where my partner works as chief engineer. Our production company's offices are in the same building. My partner does most of the administration and writes most of the lyrics, which is great for me because I just show up and compose. I get the lyrics, play what I hear, and we go from there. Typically we'll record a demo first. Ninety percent of the time there's a good reaction to the demo, so we go back to the studio and finish it up. Typically the things are written one day, recorded on another and maybe mixed the next. Then it's on to the next project.

What do you like most about your work?
I really like being able to write something and be finished

with it days later. It's fun to move on to something else. Also, it's very rewarding to deal with the whole range of musical styles.

What do you like least?
There's not a lot of job security. But by the time you've been in music for 10 or 20 years, you either get used to it or you do something else.

What's your proudest achievement?
No one thing. I just feel fortunate that I can do the kinds of things I'm doing and make a living at it.

What advice would you offer to someone who's interested in a career as a composer?
Practical experience is the most valuable thing. Certainly, you have to have enough of the basics under your belt so that you're competent, but the experience of being out there doing things is the most valuable thing of all. Fortunately, I don't think a degree in music makes much difference in the kind of things that I'm doing. If you can write and sing, that's all that really matters. There's always going to be a market for that.

RECORDING ENGINEER

Whoever first said, "That's music to my ears," might well have been a satisfied recording engineer. Before it can be preserved in a recording, music passes by the sharp ears and skillful hands of a recording engineer. Seated behind a huge console and surrounded by blinking lights, the engineer makes sure that the sounds on tape are as good—or better—than the actual sounds of the performance.

A few decades ago recording engineers came from technical backgrounds in electronics and acoustics. With the rock-and-roll boom of the sixties, the field became a haven for technically inclined musicians, and today most recording engineers begin with an interest in music. However, the field is becoming more technical once again as synthesizers, sequencers, computers, automated mixing consoles, digital recording and other high-tech developments become widespread. It's not uncommon today for aspiring engineers to get some technical training at a specialized recording school.

Whatever your background, however, you're likely to start as a "gofer" at a recording studio. Then you'll become an assistant engineer and finally a full-fledged engineer. The job requires intense concentration and attention to detail and the ability to work closely with producers and musicians. Many of the skills required for the job are also valuable for work in radio, television, film and video production and live concert sound, although these are distinct fields with their own technical requirements.

If you're in charge of your band's sound system, or if you make recordings of your own music at home, you might consider looking further into this career. You can get a bird's-eye view of the field by taking a job as a receptionist or gofer at a local studio. If you like what you see—and hear—perhaps you'll find that the pressures of the career are more than compensated for by the rewards of participating in the creation of great music.

What You Need to Know

- ❑ Audio recording (the process and functions of various devices)
- ❑ Audio and control interfacing (the interaction of signals among the various machines in the studio)
- ❑ Computerized music production and MIDI (musical instrument digital interface) technology (the process and functions of various devices)
- ❑ Basic concepts of analog and digital audio technology
- ❑ Audio theory (the nature of sound)
- ❑ Basic musical concepts and terminology
- ❑ The sonic characteristics of various musical instruments and styles
- ❑ The "sound" of popular records from various eras
- ❑ Basic concepts of video (which often accompanies audio)

Necessary Skills

- ❑ Ability to operate all recording studio equipment
- ❑ "Good ears," the ability to hear and discriminate among sonic details
- ❑ A natural sense of rhythm, pitch and musical style
- ❑ Ability to follow a musical score (helpful in some situations)
- ❑ Soldering and other audio maintenance skills
- ❑ Analytical ability (to assess the likely cause of a technical problem)

Do You Have What It Takes?

- ❑ Ability to work as part of a team
- ❑ Good powers of concentration for long periods of time
- ❑ Patience (recording often requires many takes)
- ❑ Self-motivation and persistence
- ❑ Ability to remain calm and productive in stressful situations

Education

No formal education is necessary, but coursework in audio engineering and recording techniques is very helpful, as is training in electronics. Courses in computer literacy, MIDI and synthesis can give you a head start in learning how to use computerized music production equipment.

Training in all subject areas of music (performance, music theory, music history, orchestration, arrangement, harmony, counterpoint, composition, etc.) is helpful for communicating with musicians and understanding the musical requirements of a given project.

Licenses Required

None

Job Outlook

Competition for jobs: quite competitive

New technology means that high-quality recordings can be made in low-cost facilities or even at home. The result is less business for recording studios and fewer staff positions for recording engineers. Now most engineers are freelancers. At the same time, the proliferation of schools for recording engineering has created a glut of well-qualified hopefuls.

The bright side is that as the number of home studios and similar small facilities increases, it will open a large, if not very wealthy, market for engineers. In addition, changes in technology are creating a demand for new skills such as digital editing. The key to a recording engineer's success in the future will be flexibility, a broad base of contacts and hands-on familiarity with a wide variety of equipment.

The Ground Floor

Entry-Level Jobs

❑ Gofer
❑ Tape-copy engineer
❑ Assistant engineer

Virtually every engineer starts as a gofer—running errands, answering the phone, managing the tape library, keeping the coffee pot filled and generally being helpful. Very large studios, and those connected with a major record label, sometimes have a tape-copy room that may be staffed by aspiring engineers.

You can graduate rather quickly to the status of assistant engineer, also called a second engineer or tape operator. An assistant helps the engineer in any way required and may also be responsible for light maintenance. When working under a freelance engineer, an assistant is expected to know how to configure and operate all of the studio's equipment.

Beginners (assistant engineers)

◆ **On-the-Job Responsi-bilities**

- ❏ May align tape machines (calibrating tape decks for optimal performance)
- ❏ Set up microphones, cables, chairs, music stands, etc. before sessions and any equipment required during sessions
- ❏ Document contents of tape reels during sessions
- ❏ Start and stop any tape machines not remote controlled by the engineer
- ❏ Oversee any tape copies that need to be made after sessions
- ❏ Put away equipment after sessions

Experienced Recording Engineers

- ❏ Consult with the producer to map out a strategy for the project
- ❏ Oversee all recording procedures and operate all studio equipment
- ❏ Select and position microphones and position instruments for basic recording and make sure all sounds are recorded properly
- ❏ Organize and execute overdubs (additions to the basic recording)

When You'll Work

❑ Determine levels and balances for the final mix (in which all instruments and other sounds are combined)
❑ Assemble finished mixes in the proper order for release

A busy recording studio may be booked 24 hours a day every day, and the staff must accommodate that schedule. Sessions usually last between three and six hours but may be open ended—you work as long as the client requires. Both staffers and freelance engineers routinely work on weekends and holidays. Advertising clients tend to do their recording during normal business hours, but the scheduling for rock, country, jazz, rap, dance and other types of popular music is extraordinarily unstructured.

Time Off

Assistant engineers are usually on staff, so their vacations are dependent on the employer's policy. They may be given a few days off or a few weeks, which may or may not be paid. Assistants are teamed with specific producers and engineers and may not be able to go on vacation if their team has work to do. The situation for staff engineers is the same. Freelancers, of course, can vacation whenever they wish.

Slack seasons aren't consistent from year to year. There tends to be one in early winter, after advertisers and record companies have prepared their holiday releases.

Perks

❑ Free or discounted access to studio equipment during unbooked hours
❑ Free access to new equipment for a trial period
❑ "Special thanks" or other credit on compact disc covers (occasionally)
❑ Free services of musicians for personal recording projects (possibly)
❑ Free compact discs (occasionally)
❑ Free admission to concerts (occasionally)
❑ Health insurance benefits for studio staff employees (in some cases)

❏ Recording studios
❏ Mobile recording facilities
❏ Music production companies
❏ Tape duplicators
❏ Private customers who maintain home studios

Beginners: little opportunity for travel.

However, if you work for a mobile recording facility, you may travel continually, but the schedule is usually grueling.

Experienced professionals: good potential for travel.

Freelance engineers who work for established recording artists often travel frequently. Most top studios are in Los Angeles, New York, Nashville or London; the most exclusive are built on Caribbean islands, in medieval European castles, on sprawling ranches and other exotic locations— reserved, of course, for projects with large budgets.

Recording studios usually consist of a large room in which musicians play, known as the studio or live room, and a smaller one housing the necessary equipment, called the control room. The engineer is usually confined to the control room, seated behind a mixing console for hours at a time. Most control rooms are cramped but air conditioned. Dim lighting is fashionable in the control room.

Depending on playback levels, the studio can be very noisy, which brings the potential of ear damage over the long term.

Starting salary: up to $20,000 yearly
After five years: $15,000 to $50,000 yearly
Top earners: unlimited for very successful freelancers

It is common for assistants to be on staff, while engineers work directly for producers on a freelance basis. Many studios offer staff positions in which engineers and assistants work exclusively for the facility, but on an hourly, on-call basis, often without a guaranteed minimum.

Pay scales for staff jobs vary widely depending on how successful the facility is and whether the employer offers a guaranteed salary (as opposed to an hourly wage), medical benefits, overtime pay and paid vacation. The more generous the benefits, the lower the pay is likely to be. Gofers often work for free until they are promoted to assistant status.

In general, freelancers command a higher hourly wage than staffers, although it still may be quite low. The most successful few—those whose records consistently reach the Top Ten—may receive as much as $5,000 per day and may be booked months in advance. In addition, engineers may receive extra money from successful producers for a job well done.

Moving Up

Recording engineers move up the ladder—from assistant to staff engineer, to chief engineer, to perhaps running their own studio—by gaining experience and credits and by taking the initiative to acquire ever-greater responsibilities. Advancement is based on talent, skill and consistent performance. Working for famous clients or being associated with success of any kind can speed the process.

Familiarity with a wide variety of recording equipment is essential. Recording technology changes so fast that the details of any particular experience quickly become outdated. Those lucky enough to have access to state-of-the-art equipment have a great advantage. Manufacturer-sponsored courses designed for maintenance personnel may be helpful. And keeping on top of new musical styles and sounds and knowing how to create them sharpens an engineer's competitive edge.

Where the Jobs Are

The most jobs—and heaviest competition—for recording engineers in the U.S. are in the major music industry centers: Los Angeles, Nashville, Chicago and New York. Major recording studios can also be found in Minneapolis, San Francisco, Austin, Dallas, Atlanta and other large cities. In cities such as Detroit, Philadelphia, Seattle, Denver, Memphis, New Orleans and Miami, recording studio owners are likely to double as recording engineer, studio manager and accountant, so opportunities are more limited.

Some recording goes on in just about every part of the country, if only for local advertising and rock groups. If you are determined, you'll probably be able to find entry-level or entrepreneurial opportunities in your area.

The music industry, particularly its more technical areas, is dominated by men. Although there's no obvious disadvantage to being a woman in this field, a fraternity atmosphere prevails at most recording studios. Nonetheless, female recording engineers are not unheard of, and more women are entering the field. Many smaller facilities are owned and managed by husband-and-wife teams.

◆ **The Male/Female Equation**

The Bad News
❑ Long, unpredictable work hours
❑ Job often interferes with personal life
❑ Stressful and cramped working conditions
❑ Low pay in many situations

The Good News
❑ The excitement of making music
❑ Creative environment, constant challenge
❑ Opportunity to work with state-of-the-art music technology
❑ Possibility of working with well-known musicians
❑ Possibility (however small) of very high pay

◆ **Making Your Decision: What to Consider**

Audio Engineering Society (AES)
60 East 42nd Street
New York, New York 10165
212-661-8528

◆ **More Information Please**

This organization sponsors semiannual conventions (open to nonmembers) that feature seminars and workshops dealing with professional issues.

National Academy of Recording Arts and Sciences (NARAS)
303 North Glenoaks Boulevard, M-140
Burbank, California 91502
213-849-1313

Write or call for a free copy of "The Grammy in the Schools Career Handbook" and a reprint from *Mix* magazine, "Readin', Writin' and Recordin'; The Basics of Finding a Recording School."

WHAT IT'S REALLY LIKE

Questar Welsh, 32,
freelance recording engineer,
Brooklyn, New York
Years in the business: 16

What's your musical background?
In high school I taught myself how to play the piano with a Beatles chord book. I learned guitar the same way, with records and books. I never took music lessons besides those I got from singing in the choir.

How did you break into recording engineering?
I went to a small studio in Brooklyn Heights to play for an artist that I'd met. I hit it off with the owner, who was also the engineer. Actually being in the studio blew my mind, so I asked him if he would teach me. I went in every day and worked on his sessions, and he taught me everything he knew. It was an education I could never have gotten in school; he saved me years of having to struggle to figure things out by myself. He said, "Use this place as though it were your own." I'd go in there on a Friday night and not come out until Sunday night. I'd work on my own music, experiment, go nuts. Within six months I was doing ses-

sions, and within two years I was freelancing, doing record dates all over the city.

If I got an opportunity to work somewhere else, the studio owner never held me back. I started doing all different kinds of things. I started working for small rap labels, so I was at the cutting edge of rap music for a few years. Eventually, I put together my own studio at home.

Was that the usual way to get started?
Not really. I didn't start out as a gofer. Well, I was a gofer, but I was in the control room, not making coffee.

Do you have any technical background?
No. I used to try to fix my guitar pedals and that kind of stuff. That was it.

What was the hardest aspect of being a recording engineer during your first couple of years?
I worked 20 hours at a stretch, but it didn't bother me because I was learning. So probably the hardest part was the money, because when I started out, I wasn't making any. Thank God I had some saved up.

How long did it take you to get established?
About two years, which is really fast. I was fortunate—I was in the right place at the right time and I had enough talent and smarts to be around people who were making it.

What do you currently do?
I've recorded the Orange Bowl half-time shows for the past four years, and I've been doing record dates for people like Chubb Rock. I've evolved into more of a composer/producer. As home studios became the big thing, the clients I had who became successful and made money went out and bought the same recording equipment that I have. So now I have to find something else to keep me eating. The record business is in real rough shape. There aren't a lot of dates around, and 10 percent of the people are doing 90 percent of the work.

What do you like most about your work as a recording engineer?
I like to see an idea become something tangible—such as developing drum parts and bass lines, textures within the sound. Today, a lot of engineers are synthesizer and MIDI

programmers as well. I got into that early on. I've always been on the creative side rather than strictly technical.

What do you like least?
Freelance hours. I've gotten tired of midnight sessions that last until eight in the morning. You lose two days on a midnight session—that day and the next one, too. Unless you don't mind being a vegetable.

What's your proudest achievement?
Believe it or not, it's making a living strictly in the music business for 16 years and not needing to work a day job, drive a cab, wait tables.

What advice would you give to someone considering a career in recording engineering?
Every day I go into a new state-of-the-art studio, and it has a new piece of equipment that I have no idea how to use. And by the time I know how to use it, there's something new. The only thing I can say is: Don't fall behind for an instant.

Leslie Ann Jones, 41,
staff recording engineer,
Capitol Recording Studios,
Los Angeles, California
Years in the business: 15

Do you have a musical background?
I used to be a guitarist and singer. I stopped when I started doing sound work. But I've managed to keep up some of my music reading skills, which really helps at the moment.

How does reading music help you as a recording engineer?
I recorded a string section with record producer David Foster. When he's telling the conductor about where he wants to start or fix a part, he speaks in terms of bar numbers. If I didn't read music, he would have to tell me what's going on all the time. It's one of the things that has contributed to my advancing rapidly in this field. Having some musical knowledge is as important as being computer literate now. You really have to have both.

How did you break into this field?

The band that I was in did a lot of recording, although nothing was ever released. I got the PA system when we broke up. I decided that I didn't have what it took to be a great guitar player, but I had an affinity for recording and sound. I started doing sound for other groups and eventually formed a company with a couple of friends who also had some PA equipment. We bought a four-track tape machine and a console, put it in my basement and started doing recordings. I took some courses in recording engineering taught by one of the guys who had engineered sessions for my former band. That gave me the opportunity to ask a lot of questions and learn.

What was your first job?

I got a job with ABC Recording Studios in the tape-copy room. Record companies need to supply their foreign affiliates and licensees with tape copies of material they're going to release. So the work involved taking the final copy of the master tape, which is basically the way the final record will sound, and copying that and sending it to Japan or wherever. I also did a lot of cassette dubs. I was on a regular shift, doing nothing but making tape copies, from 5 P.M. until about one in the morning. I did tape copies for about six months, then I became an assistant engineer. That lasted about a year, until I started doing overdubs for other engineers and things like that. After about two years there, I did my first album.

Is it usual to start in the tape-copy room?

It's one way to start in studios that are tied to a major record label. Independent studios don't need to have that kind of facility, so most people enter as gofers.

What experiences prepared you for this career?

Having spent a lot of time in the music end of it. Everything I did from the time I was 14 until I finally became an engineer involved some form of music. Either I was playing, or I was doing live sound, or working for a record company. I picked up every magazine and every book on recording I could find.

What was the hardest aspect of working during your first few years as a recording engineer?
Getting used to the schedule—or lack of one, to be exact. Doing 18 hours at a stretch, working weekends, that kind of stuff. It becomes your life, until you attain a level of success where you can have control over it. Also, not making a big mistake, like erasing something by accident. A lot of times you're given perhaps more responsibility than you should have, because nobody knows just how prepared you are at any given time.

What is a day's work like for you?
Well, tomorrow I'll come in at 9 and set up for a Taco Bell jingle. That runs from 10 A.M. until 3 P.M. Then I have a break. Then I'm doing a guitar/vocal demo from 5 P.M. until probably 9 or 10 at night.

What do you like most about your work?
I like being there when things happen—when somebody has been working really hard on a part and then they get it, or when somebody who's a real natural performer comes in and sings a great line. That's the best part.

What do you like least?
The lack of schedule. You never know what's coming up until the last minute. You can't expect to make a date for Friday night. If you do, you'll be continuously disappointed because you'll most likely have to cancel.

What's your proudest achievement?
Being president of the San Francisco chapter of NARAS (the National Association of Recording Arts and Sciences). That, and being one of the mixers on the Grammy Awards.

What advice would you give to someone who's thinking about a career in this field?
Have a basic knowledge of music. And become computer literate, preferably on a Macintosh. Read as much as you can and ask as many questions as you can.

Tom Garneau, 30,
staff recording engineer,
Paisley Park Recording Studios,
Minnetonka, Minnesota
Years in the business: Six

How did you break into recording engineering?
I went to an alternative school that allowed me to design
my own learning experiences. In grade school there was a
synthesizer and in junior high there was a four-track re-
corder in the choir room. I'd get permission to lock myself
in there and mess around.

When I graduated from high school, I asked my mother
how much she paid for my brother to go to college. She
said, "About five grand." I said, "Give me five grand and
let me invest it in recording equipment. If you don't like
what's happening after a year, I'll sell the stuff and give
you your money back." So I bought some equipment, built
an eight-track studio and got anybody I could to come in
and record—and, hopefully, to pay me for it.

After a few years I decided to try to make a living out of it.
I had a few friends in the music business, and I convinced
them to record with me. I started establishing a client base.
Eventually I was doing everything from albums to jingles
to soundtracks for audio-visual presentations to songwriting
demos.

**What was the hardest aspect of working in this field
during your first few years?**
When I had my own company, it was the uncertainty. Am I
going to be able to pay the rent? Am I going to have to get
a job at McDonald's? But something always popped up in
the nick of time.

What do you currently do?
These days I do a lot of mixing. Most mixdown sessions
are booked for 24 hours a day. Nobody can really work 24
hours a day, but a lot of them seem to want to try. You have
to make a choice about whether you'll start at the same
time every day or begin work later and later, for instance,
starting at 2 P.M. and working until 6 A.M., and then starting

the next session at 4 P.M. and working until 8 A.M. If you do that, after a while your schedule just revolves around the clock. When I'm on that kind of project I might work for 16 hours a day or more for three or four weeks, with a day off every once in a while. When it's over, I have a couple of weeks off, if the schedule permits. I've also worked with producers who keep "banker's hours" for rock and roll—they'll only work between 2 P.M. and 10 P.M. Monday through Friday.

What do you most like about your work?
It's very creative. Every record I work on, I'm bringing something to the party. There are aspects of the record that sound the way they do because of me. I can work 100 hours a week and still I drive home saying "I love my job!"

What do you like least?
The long hours, the low pay. Some clients are unreasonable. They have to rain on the parade continually because of ego, inexperience or a bad attitude. It can be such a pleasant experience, but some people just don't get it.

What's your proudest achievement?
It's always the latest thing I've done. The M.C. Hammer record I mixed last year went to Number Two (*Too Legit to Quit*), and so far it's sold triple platinum (platinum is one million units sold). I'm not a big rap fan, but I'm able to look through any style and find something that I can contribute. It doesn't really matter what I'm working on.

What advice would you give to someone who wants to be a recording engineer?
You can't really have a choice in the matter—it has to be so much a part of you that you can't do anything else. If the desire isn't that deep, you won't be able to cut it. Employers have their pick from the cream of the crop, and they can see that spark. And you need that spark in the beginning, when you're working 18 hours a day at the bottom of the totem pole doing all of the crap. If you don't love it, you'll be quitting soon.

Musicians have always needed instruments. But today, not only performers but composers, arrangers, copyists, producers and recording engineers depend on a bewildering array of equipment, from traditional instruments to MIDI (musical instrument digital interface) sequencers and digital audio workstations. Musical equipment salespeople provide all these people with the tools they need.

People interested in this career path usually begin with some musical ability—indeed, for some it's a way of supplementing a meager income as a performer. Many musicians find the excitement of making a sale, not to mention the opportunity to get their hands on the latest gear, as satisfying as their musical endeavors. A sales career generally offers both higher pay and greater job security as well.

Selling musical gear is certainly less competitive than performing or writing songs for a living, but it does have its own challenges and pressures. As a retail salesperson, your income is based on the amount of equipment you sell, so earning power is determined entirely by the quality of your performance. Your paycheck can vary wildly from month to month, and pressures from your employer can be intense. But the opportunity to succeed is open to anyone, regardless of educational background or musical skill. All it takes is a flair for selling and the dedication to make it work for you.

You're likely to start as a clerk or cashier at a music store. Once you've learned the ropes, you'll be assigned to one of the store's departments. Through training meetings and on-the-job experience, you'll learn how to serve customers and close a sale. From there, you may graduate to a management position. If you're really ambitious and have a head for business, you might eventually open your own store.

If you understand musicians and their concerns, love musical instruments and equipment, and have good people skills, you might consider trying an entry-level job at a music store. You'll know before long if you're in tune with the demands of this career.

What You Need to Know

❏ Basic musical terminology and concepts
❏ Basic retail sales concepts and techniques
❏ Operation of the instruments and devices offered by your store or department

For those who are dealing with electric or electronic equipment:

❏ Basic concepts in analog and digital electronics
❏ Audio and control interfacing (the interaction of signals among the various electronic musical devices)

For those who are selling recording systems:

❏ Audio recording (the process and functions of various devices)

For those who are selling software and/or keyboards:

❏ Computerized music production and MIDI technology (the process and functions of various devices)

Necessary Skills

❏ Play an instrument
❏ Ability to keep accurate, legible records
❏ Ability to read and interpret equipment-operation manuals
❏ Trouble-shooting (the ability to assess the likely cause of an instrument's technical problem)
❏ Ability to design and position in-store displays

Do You Have What It Takes?

❏ Upbeat attitude
❏ Self-motivation
❏ Outgoing personality, gift of gab
❏ Good listening skills (an effective sales pitch requires understanding a customer's needs)
❏ Ability to relate to working musicians
❏ Persistence (you may have to deal with a customer several times before you make a sale)
❏ Even temperament (you have to keep smiling even when customers get difficult)

❑ A thick skin; your best efforts may *not* result in a sale

❑ Ability to work as part of a team

Education

No formal education is necessary, but training in instrumental/vocal or ensemble performance (playing as part of a group) is recommended. Courses in audio recording are helpful for learning how to use recording equipment. Courses in computer literacy, MIDI and synthesis are very helpful in learning how to use computer-based music production equipment. Courses in electronics and shop are helpful in preparation for setting up equipment and displays.

Job Outlook

◆ Licenses Required

None

Competition for jobs: slightly competitive

The late eighties witnessed a revolution in the technologies of performing, composing and recording music that drastically boosted sales, particularly of high-ticket electronic instruments and recording equipment. Still, the recession of the early nineties has had a dire effect on musical equipment retailing. Musical instrument stores are also threatened by mail-order retailers, who can offer instruments and equipment at lower prices than stores can afford to do.

New musical technologies will continue to develop, stimulating sales. Compared to many other music-related fields, sales is far less competitive, although within the retailing community itself competition is quite fierce. Salespeople who keep up with new technologies and can explain and demonstrate them to customers will have the most success in the future.

Entry-level jobs: salesperson, sales clerk or cashier, or shipping and receiving person

◆ **The Ground Floor**

◆ **On-the-Job Responsibilities**

Beginners

- ❑ Stock shelves
- ❑ Take inventory
- ❑ Carry items from the stock room to the sales floor
- ❑ Build displays
- ❑ Keep the sales floor and displays neat and attractive
- ❑ Sell small items such as cables, guitar strings, recording tape, instructional books and miscellaneous accessories
- ❑ Take payments, operate the cash register and bag purchases
- ❑ Assist senior salespeople in any way necessary
- ❑ Take merchandise off trucks, unpack it and place it on inventory shelves (shipping and receiving person)

Experienced Salespeople

- ❑ Oversee all sales and make sure the customer is satisfied
- ❑ Attend sales meetings to discuss strategies and to practice techniques
- ❑ Make telephone calls to prospective customers
- ❑ Provide customer support, answering technical questions and trouble-shooting equipment problems
- ❑ Demonstrate products
- ❑ Design merchandise displays
- ❑ Design and assemble music production and recording systems
- ❑ Organize and oversee special marketing and promotional events
- ❑ Visit large prospective customers
- ❑ Oversee installation of new equipment in client facilities
- ❑ Act as liaison between customers and manufacturers

When You'll Work

Musical equipment salespeople often work more than five days a week and eight hours a day. Stores usually stay open on weekends and well into the evening, and employers generally don't allow much flexibility in their staff's schedules. Music stores are busiest during the winter holidays and early summer, when students are free to think about playing music. Overtime is the norm during these times.

For special customers (usually prominent musicians or recording facilities), the store might arrange special after-hours demonstrations for which salespeople must be on hand. Likewise, special clients may require house calls during odd hours or on weekends. In addition, there are installations, trade shows, recording sessions and other special events to attend.

Time Off

Most stores offer at least a week's paid vacation. Federal holidays are big shopping days and aren't normally free, but major holidays tend to be observed. Salespeople may be able to choose their vacation days as long as they don't fall during the busiest times.

Perks

- ❏ Free access to the latest musical equipment
- ❏ Free musical merchandise (occasionally)
- ❏ Discounts on musical merchandise
- ❏ Free promotional items (T-shirts, caps and the like)
- ❏ Free admission to concerts and other events
- ❏ Opportunity to meet prominent musicians
- ❏ Possible opportunity to freelance for store clients as a consultant, MIDI programmer, performer or recording engineer
- ❏ Health insurance benefits for store employees (in some cases)

Who's Hiring

- ❏ Musical instrument stores (which cater primarily to musicians)
- ❏ Professional audio supply stores (which cater primarily to recording studios, sound reinforcement outfits

and production companies)

❏ Studio consulting and installation services (which cater primarily to recording studios and performance spaces)

Beginners: no travel potential

◆ **Places You'll Go**

Experienced professionals: potential for regular travel. When you've gained enough experience and developed a range of contacts in the musical community, you can expect to travel regularly. You're likely to visit facilities and musicians in various cities within your region, either to demonstrate new equipment, deliver large orders or provide after-sales support. You'll also travel across the U.S. to attend special training seminars offered by manufacturers or to industry trade association annual conventions. The latter usually take place in Los Angeles, New York, Las Vegas, Atlanta, Chicago and in Frankfurt, Germany.

◆ **Surroundings**

Salespeople are often confined to their department, which means spending long hours sharing a relatively small space with huge racks of merchandise. Stores that cater to the professional audio market (recording studios and the like) tend to be more spacious and comfortably furnished. If you visit potential clients, you'll probably spend a lot of time in the high-tech world of recording studios.

◆ **Dollars and Cents**

Retail sales is an uncertain way to earn a living. Usually a salesperson receives a basic salary, which tends to be low ($1,000 to $1,500 per month, or the legal minimum wage per hour). The rest must be earned in commissions (15 to 20 percent of the purchase price of each item sold). The salary is considered an advance against commissions; that is, you must "pay it back" to the store out of commissions before you can earn more money.

This system provides great incentive to sell as much as possible—you sink or swim solely on the basis of your ability to sell. The store also depends on moving merchandise out the door, so your performance is constantly monitored and evaluated, creating further pressure.

If you're successful, however, you'll have virtually unlimited earning potential. As you gain experience, you may be given the opportunity to sell higher-priced items, so your commission increases as well. If you're promoted to department (or store) manager, you may earn a percentage of your department's (or the store's) overall sales in addition to your own commissions.

Moving Up

Once you've graduated from an entry-level job to full salesperson, you'll work in a particular department. If you show a flair for management, you may be promoted to department manager. Eventually you may manage the entire store. The next step, if you choose, is to open your own shop. This, of course, requires a large capital investment and carries a high degree of risk.

Progress up the ladder is largely a matter of individual motivation and talent. In sales, the sole qualification for success is the ability to exchange the store's merchandise for customers' cash. Moving up to management requires thorough knowledge of the business, good judgment and the ability to motivate the sales staff.

Where the Jobs Are

Virtually every sizeable community has a musical instrument store. Large cities are likely to have several, catering to every nook and cranny of the music industry. Los Angeles, New York, Nashville and Chicago host the largest populations of musicians and support most of the recording activity in the U.S. Nonetheless, lots of music is made elsewhere, and many sound reinforcement companies, recording studios and personal studios are located in unlikely places. Wherever music is made, there's likely to be an equipment retailer nearby.

The Male/Female Equation

Men far outnumber women in music stores, reflecting the music industry as a whole. As the sexes become better integrated at all levels of the music business, the gender balance in retail stores is likely to become more equal.

MUSICAL EQUIPMENT SALESPERSON

The Bad News
❏ Earning money on a commission basis is very stressful
❏ Rejection is common-place (failing to make a sale)
❏ Performance is constantly monitored and evaluated
❏ Some customers can be ignorant and difficult to please
❏ Long work hours

The Good News
❏ Earning potential is virtually unlimited
❏ The route to success is well defined
❏ Opportunity to work with state-of-the-art equipment
❏ Opportunity to meet well-known musicians
❏ Informal dress and manners on the job

◆ **Making Your Decision: What to Consider**

Joel Faddol, 36,
musical equipment salesperson,
Al Nalli Music,
Ann Arbor, Michigan
Years in the business: 16

How did you get into selling musical instruments?
In 1976 some friends and I started a recording studio,
which later grew into three studios. I also had a job selling
home stereo systems, and I was trying to go to college,
too. My hours got completely out of hand. But the studio
business eventually collapsed, and I was left with nothing.
I had dropped out of college to do the studio thing, so I
went back into sales at a music store. Each day I would
hang out in a different department, learning about the various instruments and how to sell them.

What was your first job?
I worked for an electronics store in the Midwest. They sold
electronic parts, CB radios, TV antennas and some stereo
equipment. I learned the basics of selling there. Whenever
there was a spare moment, I would ask questions such as:
"How did you get that guy to buy that?" It was my biggest

thrill when I finally sold a couple on a stereo system for the first time. I felt like I had graduated—I knew that I could do it.

What's your musical background?
I'm a keyboardist. I've been playing jazz since I was in college, rock since I was in high school, and I've taken lessons since I was a kid. Right now I'm playing in a progressive reggae band.

What was the hardest aspect of working in this field during your first few years?
The rejection. It really gets to you. I'm a performer at heart—most salespeople are. Sales is just like any other performance, and you have a certain amount of performer's pride in what you do. And if you blew the sale, then obviously you didn't perform well. It also comes down to money. You make your money on commission, so a rejection means that your dinner just walked out of the store.

What do you do in a day's work?
I'm in a unique situation. Although I'm associated with a store, I work out of my own basement. First I get a lead, either from the store or from the manufacturing representatives. Then I call you, explain how I got your name and what I sell and find out what your needs might be. I try to set up an appointment at your facility, and if you're interested, I'll set up a demo for you. If I do sell you something, you can be sure that I'm not going to retire on that; I want all of your business for all eternity. So I'll keep in touch. I'll ask for recommendations, friends of yours that I can call. If I run into someone who's involved in music, I'll give him a card and contact him.

What do you like most about your work?
I love being in all the studios. My heart races when I see knobs and buttons, switches and sliders. I get my hands on all the cool gear!

What do you like least?
I don't get enough money for the amount of work that I do. The profits are relatively low. Competition is outrageous. Very few product lines give me anything like an exclusive, which means that I have competition around the block,

across the state, across the country, even internationally. It's relentless.

What is your proudest achievement?
Staying in the business. We've lost a lot of music dealers in this state in the past few years. I'm not dancing on their graves; I hate to see anyone going through that. And it's true that if my boss couldn't hang, then I couldn't hang. But he certainly couldn't do it without me, either.

What advice would you offer someone who's interested in a career in musical equipment sales?
Get a good grasp of both electronics and music. This is a highly technical field—almost everything has a computer in it. There are any number of functions available on any piece, and you have to know what they are and how they relate to the customer's line of work. If I'm trying to sell a digital editing system to a video postproduction house and all I know about is music editing, I might as well not be doing the demo. One day I have to discuss MIDI synthesizers, the next day it's a touring PA system and the next it's a 24-track recording console. If you're going to sell this stuff, you have to be ready to sell to everybody.

David Shymatta, 24,
musical equipment salesperson,
Goodman Music,
Los Angeles, California
Years in the business: four

How did you get started in musical equipment sales?
I was going to Grove School of Music in Los Angeles. I figured that since I was heading toward a career in music, I would apply for a job at a music store. I had intended it to be temporary, but I've been doing it ever since.

What was your first job?
I worked at Guitar Center in Sherman Oaks. I spent most of the time learning basic sales techniques, but I learned a lot about keyboards, too. There's new technology all the time, and you have to stay on top of it. After about a

year and a half, I was put in charge of the entire keyboard department.

Was that a usual way to start?
Yeah, in that I got into it from the musical end, rather than from sales. You rarely see people working in music stores who are really equipped in sales. It's mostly musicians. But a lot of them become totally dedicated to the sales part of it.

What happens in a day's work?
Usually it's a little slow in the morning, so I spend that time making follow-up calls—I get back to people who called with a question the previous day. You have to deal with a lot of technical questions, especially in the keyboard department. Answering someone's question might determine whether they buy from you or from someone else. Later, people come in to check out the things I've told them about. I'm usually on the sales floor until 7:30 or 8:00 at night. It makes sense to stay as late as possible, because the longer you're there, the more chance you have to sell something. Every now and then we do a special consultation after hours at the store or the customer's house.

What was the hardest aspect of doing this job during your first year?
You really have to go the extra mile—you can't ever ease up. You have to keep making calls. You can't sit down too much. You have to be creative, and you have to be able to improvise. A lot of times you can turn a situation around just by doing a few extra little things. A customer might say, "I want to buy a synthesizer." But if what he really wants to do is write songs, you might be able to sell him a sequencer or a computer, too.

What do you like most about your work?
There's a real challenge in figuring out what customers really want. In addition to that, it's music. I write songs and do a lot of technical stuff in my spare time, and I do this for a living, so it all fits together.

What do you like least?
When it gets too busy on the sales floor—people don't get taken care of properly, and they might get the wrong impression. Also, dealing with people who aren't familiar

with the equipment. They can get so confused that it's impossible to deal with them.

What advice would you offer someone who's interested in this career?

Pay attention to little things as well as big things. It may not seem worth your while to deal with a guy who just wants to buy a cable, but he may come back, say "Thanks for the deal on that cable" and buy a $10,000 system. You just never know.

Gary Gand, 38,
president, Gand Music,
Northfield, Illinois
Years in the business: 21

How did you break into selling musical instruments?

I started playing guitar and banjo professionally when I was ten years old. In my teens, I started trading instruments. You know, I had three or four guitars, and I'd get rid of one and buy another. I discovered that I liked doing that. Eventually, I had so many guitars that I rented a place to hang them all up.

What's your musical background?

My dad was a musician during his younger years, but he made his living as a traveling salesman. When folk music became popular in the early sixties, he began playing guitar, and my sister and I did, too. We started performing as a folk trio, playing local gigs at Moose Lodges and Cub Scout dinners. Then we started playing at folk and bluegrass festivals around the country. Eventually we did some television, played Disneyland, all the state fairs and then world's fairs. After I quit playing professionally, I mixed sound for touring groups. I toured with EmmyLou Harris for a long time, and I did the last two King Crimson tours.

What was the hardest aspect of working in this business during your first few years?

Keeping the customers happy. When you're on the sales floor, it's like each of your customers is your boss. They all want it, they want it now, they want it a certain way.

You're trying to please all these people so that they'll come back and buy more from you. It's impossible to do, so you have to learn to accept your own failure without taking it personally. To this day, I still kick myself when a sale doesn't happen, or when somebody returns something a week after they've bought it.

What do you do in a day's work?
Before we open, we begin with a meeting to talk about the day's events. Then for the first few hours I'm putting out fires, mostly helping big customers who are having problems with their equipment, or dealing with manufacturers. After that, I'll work on the sales floor a little bit, maybe work on displays or answer questions from the salespeople. By 8 at night we're counting the money. Of course, throughout the month there are lots of routine things: sifting through paperwork, going over profit-and-loss statements, looking at data about slow- and fast-moving items, meetings with department managers.

What do you like most about your work?
The gear. I just love it. The stuff we sell here is really cutting edge. We're dealing with the equipment that everyone is reading about in the magazines, so we're surfing on the crest of this big wave. It's a great place to be.

What do you like least?
The pandemonium. There's a lot of wasted emotion, effort and energy in the music industry in general. There are fires to put out all of the time, and it creates a lot of anxiety. The other day, a guy came in who used to manage one of my competitors, and I asked him what he was doing now. He said, "I really couldn't handle the pressure, so now I'm an air traffic controller." He said that's a lot more mellow than managing a music store!

What advice would you offer to someone who's interested in getting into musical equipment sales?
Get yourself into a store any way you can. Get a summer job. Sweep the floors. Work for free. Just get in there, observe and ask questions. It's all on-the-job training. You can read books about sales, but learning how to do it, and how to deal with people, only comes with hands-on experience.

AUDIO MAINTENANCE TECHNICIAN

There's an impressive array of equipment in a recording studio. Someone must be on hand at all times so that precious studio time—which may amount to hundreds of dollars an hour—isn't lost to a broken tape deck or a faulty connection. This role belongs to the audio maintenance technician, or tech. If you've ever soldered cables, attempted to fix a broken stereo or built an amplifier from a kit, you're already on the road to becoming one.

Techs receive the least public exposure in the music industry. They work behind the scenes, far from the recognition that may greet the recordings made under their care. A fascination with technology and pride in a job well done are their

71

primary rewards. The job varies from the bland routine of aligning tape machines before each recording session to handling any technical emergency that might arise.

Techs are in their element when a recording session comes to a halt due to equipment failure. They have to assess the problem and deal with it calmly and quickly—all the while soothing the tempers of anxious producers, recording engineers and musicians.

Although many techs have completed coursework at a recording school or hold a two-year certificate in electronics, others learn everything they need to know on the job. Regardless of educational background, everyone must spend some time at the bottom of the ladder, performing routine maintenance, repairing simple devices such as cables, replacing basic studio components and installing new equipment. Eventually, they are responsible for trouble shooting, repairs, modifications and recording system design.

If you want to take the first step, consider an apprenticeship with a studio, tape duplication facility, audio maintenance company or a road crew (on tour with a performing group). After that you might land a staff position or perhaps have enough experience to start your own freelance business. If you're a born entrepreneur, you may eventually design and build your own high-tech recording studio.

So, in the most literal sense, how does that sound?

What You Need to Know

❑ Basic electronics—analog and digital
❑ Audio and control interfacing (the interaction of signals among the various machines in the studio)
❑ Audio recording (the process and functions of various devices)
❑ Video playback basics (often accompanies audio)

Necessary Skills

❑ How to use electronics tools (such as a volt/ohm meter and an oscilloscope)
❑ How to use machine shop tools
❑ Soldering
❑ Ability to read a circuit diagram
❑ Ability to read and interpret repair manuals
❑ Technical drawing (helpful but not required)

Do You Have What It Takes?

❑ Ability to work in relative isolation and as part of a team
❑ Patience (figuring out what the problem is and how to fix it can take time)
❑ Even temperament (you have to keep your cool even when those around you don't)
❑ Diplomacy (you have to satisfy the demands of anxious recording engineers, producers and musicians)
❑ Being methodical and organized in your work habits

Physical Attributes

❑ Good eyesight (you work with very small components)
❑ Strong back (you'll do a lot of leaning over)
❑ Excellent hearing

Education

No formal education necessary. Some training in elec-

◆ **Getting into the Field**

tronics, audio engineering and music is most helpful, as is a general background in science and mathematics.

Licenses Required

None

Job Outlook

Competition for jobs: slightly competitive

Recording facilities have been hit hard by recent changes in recording technology, which make it possible for musicians and producers to make high-quality recordings in very low-cost facilities or even at home. As a result, staff positions for maintenance technicians are less plentiful than they were only a few years ago, and this trend isn't likely to change.

On the other hand, technical maintenance remains one of the least competitive areas of the otherwise intensely competitive music industry. In addition, there are more small studios (including home studios) than ever before, and high-tech musical equipment is increasingly put to use by performing musicians as well. Skilled technicians can find work on a freelance basis or with technical maintenance companies servicing the needs of this growing community.

The Ground Floor

Entry-Level Jobs: "Gofer," technical maintenance apprentice or wire person

A gofer assists the maintenance and engineering staff in any way required: running errands, phoning in purchase orders, performing light maintenance, documenting technical problems, making coffee or straightening up the studio after sessions.

An apprentice deals with more technical matters such as cleaning patch cords. The maintenance apprentice sometimes doubles as a tape operator or assistant recording engineer, especially on mobile recording facilities. In this case he or she is responsible for starting and stopping tape machines and logging the session's results. Companies that perform studio installations often hire an entry-level wire person who is responsible for basic wiring and soldering.

Beginners

- ❏ Align tape machines (calibrating tape decks for optimal performance)
- ❏ Build, clean and repair cables and other connectors
- ❏ Repair simple devices (such as broken headphones)
- ❏ Build simple accessory devices designed by more experienced technicians

Experienced Technicians

- ❏ Trouble-shoot nonfunctional equipment
- ❏ Resolve technical emergencies
- ❏ Manage backups and spares (to quickly replace broken equipment)
- ❏ Design and build accessory devices
- ❏ Design and configure recording systems and oversee purchase of equipment

Facilities that cater to the advertising industry tend to keep nine to five, Monday-through-Friday hours, while a successful rock-, country-, rap- or jazz-oriented studio is likely to be in operation 24 hours a day every day. Of course, a maintenance technician must be on hand whenever a recording session is in progress.

Facilities that can afford an around-the-clock maintenance staff tend to stagger eight-hour shifts. On a mobile recording rig the workday is generally 12 hours long, although everyone must remain on the job until the project is finished.

Techs working a studio's late night shift must be prepared to stay until the last session has ended, which may amount to a shift much more than eight hours long. Freelancers work whenever they are called (and choose to take the job) and can expect to receive emergency calls at any hour, any day of the week.

Time Off

For staff employees vacation time varies between a few days and two weeks, which may or may not be paid. Freelancers take a vacation at their own risk: Potential clients who fail to reach you may not call back a second time.

There is no consistent slack season, although there tends to be one in early winter, after advertisers and record companies have prepared their holiday releases. Many employers honor major federal holidays, but if a client wants to work on a holiday, the studio's staff and/or stable of freelancers is expected to come in.

Perks

❑ Free access to maintenance shop, tools and test equipment
❑ Free or discount-priced access to studio equipment during unbooked hours
❑ Free records (occasionally)
❑ Free admission to concerts (occasionally)
❑ "Special thanks" or other credit on record covers (occasionally)

Who's Hiring

❑ Recording studios
❑ Audio system maintenance and installation companies
❑ Mobile recording facilities
❑ Music production companies
❑ Tape duplicators
❑ Sound reinforcement (live sound amplification) companies
❑ Touring musical and theatrical groups
❑ Radio and television stations
❑ Large theaters and performance facilities
❑ In-house media production facilities of advertising agencies, corporations, investment firms, etc.
❑ Private customers who maintain home studios

Places You'll Go

Beginners: little potential for travel.
The exception: Employees of mobile recording facilities and touring musical or theatrical groups travel constantly.

Such travel isn't envied, however, for techs don't get much time to themselves, and the schedule is often grueling. Beginners usually do the driving.

Experienced professionals: great potential for travel. Freelance techs go wherever their clients require—be it a local facility or a studio anywhere in the world. Staff techs may travel to semiannual conventions in New York, Los Angeles, Chicago, New Orleans, Atlanta and Frankfurt, Germany.

At even the plushest recording complexes, the maintenance shop tends·to get short shrift. Space is usually at a premium, and furnishings are spare. A studio's control room itself usually isn't much bigger, and the underbelly of a recording console—where a technician can expect to spend at least a little time—isn't spacious.

◆ **Surroundings**

Starting Salary: $10,000 to $20,000 yearly
After Five Years: $15,000 to $35,000 yearly
Top Earners: $30,000 to $60,000 yearly (for entrepreneurs, earning potential is unlimited)

◆ **Dollars and Cents**

Audio maintenance technicians tend to be more highly paid than recording engineers and other recording studio personnel. Still, wages are not especially generous, even at major audio facilities. (Wages for comparable work in the video field tend to be significantly higher.) Pay scales vary widely, depending on how successful the facility is and whether the employer offers a guaranteed salary, medical benefits, overtime pay and paid vacation. The more generous the benefits, the lower the pay scale is likely to be. Generally, tips and bonuses aren't a part of the deal.

Climbing the maintenance technician's ladder depends on experience, skill and talent. If you have mastered the technical aspects of the field—either in school, in manufacturer-sponsored equipment seminars or on the

◆ **Moving Up**

job—you move up by demonstrating competence and willingness to take on greater responsibilities.

Once you've developed a reputation and a track record, you might land a job as chief of maintenance at a major recording studio. The next step might be to establish a freelance business or even to open your own studio. Alternatively, through studio work, you may be hired by a major recording artist to design the artist's personal studio or touring rig. This could develop into a very high-paying freelance career servicing the special needs of prestigious clients.

Where the Jobs Are

Los Angeles, Nashville, Chicago, New York and Toronto boast the highest concentrations of facilities that hire audio maintenance technicians and therefore are the cities with the most jobs. Minneapolis, San Francisco, Austin, Dallas and Atlanta form the second tier. In cities such as Detroit, Philadelphia, Seattle, Denver, Memphis, New Orleans and Miami, the maintenance technician is also likely to be the studio owner, recording engineer, studio manager and accountant, so opportunities are more limited.

There is music recording and production going on in just about every part of the country (catering to local advertising and rock groups if nothing else). Jobs are few, but for those determined to make a career in this field, the opportunities exist.

The Male/Female Equation

Traditionally the music industry has been male turf. Over the past several years, though, women have become more visible in recording studios, and a small number of them pursue a career in technical maintenance.

The Bad News
- ❏ Low starting pay
- ❏ Unpredictable work hours
- ❏ Working under pressure, often with temperamental performers and producers
- ❏ Limited opportunities for advancement

The Good News
- ❏ Working with state-of-the-art music technology
- ❏ Job security (relative to other music-related careers)
- ❏ Less competition than other jobs in the music industry
- ❏ Informal dress and manners on the job

◆ **Making Your Decision: What to Consider**

Audio Engineering Society (AES)
60 East 42nd Street
New York, New York 10165
212-661-8528

◆ **More Information Please**

This organization sponsors semiannual conventions (open to nonmembers) that feature seminars and workshops dealing with professional issues.

National Academy of Recording Arts and Sciences (NARAS)
303 North Glenoaks Boulevard, M-140

WHAT IT'S REALLY LIKE

Paul Prestopino, 53,
freelance audio maintenance technician,
Roosevelt, New Jersey
Years in the business: 23

Do you have a musical background?
I was always a musical kid. My mother took up guitar when
I was about eight or nine, and I started learning along with
her. I started to teach myself from her folk records. That
expanded into bluegrass, into banjo, mandolin and dobro.
One day I got a call from the management of the Chad
Mitchell Trio, who had gotten my name from a friend of
mine. I worked behind Chad Mitchell for almost seven
years. When the group faded, I slid right into the recording
business.

What's your technical background?
Very scanty. I spent a year at Carnegie Tech in the physics
department. When I left school I was looking for something
to do and soon found myself working in the physics department at Princeton University as a lab technician and then
for the Kimberly-Clark Paper Company in Wisconsin. For
a year and a half I went to a machine shop course; I learned
a lot there and ended up with a two-year certificate. Then I

went to work for the University of Wisconsin's physics department. From there I got into the music business.

How did you start doing technical maintenance?

On the road with the Chad Mitchell Trio, I got involved with the sound system. When the sound guy left, I took his place, playing each night with a mixer under my chair. We did about ten albums during the time I was with them. The last one was done in an eight-track studio, which was the newest thing at the time. Until then the recordings never sounded as good as I thought we had played, but this time it came out better than what we had played. I was knocked out! I went to the recording engineer and asked, "How do I get into this?" As it turns out, he was Phil Ramone (who went on to produce hit records by Billy Joel and others). He was running a two-week workshop on recording at the Eastman School of Music. It was unbelievable; I've never learned more in the space of two weeks than I did at that workshop. When I came back, Phil helped me get a job at A&R Recording.

What was your first job?

A&R had an opening in the disk-mastering room (where final recordings are prepared for manufacture as LPs), so that was where I went to work. It's a wonderful combination of technical stuff and using your ears.

Was that a usual place to start?

The usual thing might be to start as a gofer or as an assistant, but there isn't really any normal way. In any case, there wasn't enough business for the mastering room, so I was on the street. I did some work as an engineer at a small studio, and then I began freelancing, doing studio wiring, console installations and so on. One day I dropped by Record Plant, and I went to work there the next day. Eventually I became the head of maintenance. I was there for the next 20 years.

How long did it take you to get established?

To me, being established is being able to handle whatever comes up. By the time I got to Record Plant, I was in my late twenties, and all of that previous experience—on the road, disk mastering, physics labs—enabled me to move fairly quickly. Within a few years I was as competent as anyone in the place.

How many different jobs have you held in this field?
I was at A&R Recording, which is now defunct, for a year and then Record Plant, which is also defunct. Now I'm freelance, though most of what I do is for Record Plant Remote, which is what Record Plant's mobile recording truck became after the studio went bankrupt.

What do you currently do?
For Record Plant Remote my job involves interfacing the truck with tape machines and noise reduction systems and so forth, aligning tape machines and noise reduction units and acting as tape operator (assistant recording engineer)— an unusual thing for a maintenance technician, but the norm in remote recording. Interfacing other peoples' equipment with the truck is a big job; you have to be able to think clearly to make it all work. I also design and build the interfaces between our own machines and the truck.

What do you like most about your work?
It's never the same thing two weeks in a row. Of course, there's a lot of routine work to do. Somebody has to align those tape machines every day, if not more. It's incredibly boring. But if you have your head on straight, it also gives you the time to pick up on incipient problems before they happen during a session.

What do you like least?
I have mixed feelings about people asking for special things. If it's something that can be done, and if the person asks in the right way and you know that it's going to make their lives easier, then it's a pleasure to be able to go into the shop, whip something up and hand it to them the following day. On the other hand, people ask for all kinds of impossible things. You can't tell them, "That's idiotic!" Having to be politic can be very wearing. You have to be politic at the place you work as well. If you make some little mistake, you may be out on the street the next day because the people above you don't understand that people do make mistakes. Dealing with bad management is very trying.

What advice would you give to someone who's interested in this career?
The single most important thing is to be observant—for instance, to align the tape machine with your "third eye" open, looking for problems; to be able to walk into a situation and know "what's wrong with this picture." In other words, fine tune your powers of observation. That, and learn everything you can. All of it is going to be useful at one time or another.

Eddie Ciletti, 36,
president, Manhattan Sound Technicians,
New York, New York
Years in the business: 17

Do you have a musical background?
I've always loved music; I had a phonograph at age three. I played the trombone for six years. I'm self-taught on keyboards and trumpet, and I play a little drums. Over the last few years I've also gotten into MIDI programming. I make recordings of my own music at home.

What's your technical background?
My father worked for Philco, so when I grew up there was always a TV in the house. I watched my father change vacuum tubes and other electronic components without any test equipment. I went to a special class on Saturdays at the public school where we learned all about vacuum tubes. Much later I got an associate degree in electrical engineering technology from Penn State. That kind of background was really helpful in developing a scientific approach to solving problems. I also took one class in BASIC computer programming at New York University.

How did you break into audio maintenance?
I lied, kicked and screamed my way into my first job, which was going on tour with Hall and Oates. A friend told me about a management company that was looking for a technician. The first time I went for an interview, they weren't interested. But I found out that they were looking for a backup band, so I started bringing my friends' bands

in to audition. I would call them constantly and say, "Look, I know you don't want to hire me, but if you change your mind, I'm still interested in the job." Eventually they took me on.

What were your responsibilities with Hall and Oates?
I was a roadie, a keyboard technician. I tuned the keyboards every day, and I did setup, wiring, and I did the maintenance.

Was that a usual first job?
It was at the time. It was easier to get a roadie's gig than a studio gig in those days. There were more bands touring than there were studios; now I think it's the other way around.

What do you currently do?
I have my own business, Manhattan Sound Technicians. We primarily service and install audio equipment, but we've branched out into doing light computer and light video work. At least 50 percent of my time is spent on administration of the company rather than on the technical work.

What do you like most about your work?
I find great satisfaction in replacing a $3 component or the $200 power supply and saying, "Yeah, I saved some money and I made it work."

What do you like least?
The fact that most people put their systems together by themselves, without any prior knowledge. I have to open a can of worms almost every time I go out to work on an installation.

What is your proudest achievement?
The latest is installing a Sonic Solutions digital recording system into an Apple Macintosh Quadra 900 computer. That gave me the opportunity to really get into digital interfacing and all of the different digital audio formats, including fiber optics. That technology is really sexy and mysterious. A fiber optic cable is a wire, but it's not metal—it's glass.

What advice would you give to someone interested in going into this field?

First, understand the concept of multimedia. These days audio, video, computer graphics and everything else is integrated. You can't touch one without understanding a good bit of the other. The other thing is to get as much hands-on experience as possible. Go to Radio Shack and pick up some project books. Build things and make them work. Be a tinkerer. Come to your first job with enough experience that you're ready to ask questions.

Larry Repasky, 37,
freelance technical engineer,
Nashville, Tennessee
Years in the business: 17

Do you have a musical background?

None whatsoever—though I did play accordion for a year in grade school! Between the ages of about nine and fifteen, I hung out at one of the local radio stations in Youngstown, Ohio, and fell in love with what they were doing. Because I wasn't musically adept, I thought the technical direction might be right for me.

How did you break into this field?

When I was about 15, I managed to land myself a job as janitor at a nearby recording studio.

While I was a janitor, I spent a lot of time watching and taking notes. One weekend the fellow who was doing the engineering decided that he'd rather go out on a date than stay and assemble a broadcast program. He said, "You've watched me do this. Do it." After that it became my job on a regular basis. When I was about 18, an engineer didn't show up for a commercial production session. The president of the facility said, "Jump in the hot seat." So I started doing overdubs while the engineer caught up on paperwork. I began to jump in wherever there were maintenance problems at the studio. Eventually, I was promoted to the vice presidency of that studio.

Was that a usual way to start?

People can follow two directions: They can find a facility where they can be a "gofer," or they can take courses at school. I think the latter approach leaves a lot to be desired. You'll learn how to operate the equipment, but you don't end up knowing how to get around problems.

How did you prepare yourself for technical work?

I went to a technical school and got an associate degree in electronics technology. You know, when I was in the corporate world, I was always told that I was never going to get anywhere because I didn't have a four-year degree. Well, I proved them wrong. You don't need a double-E (a bachelor's degree in electrical engineering) in order to do this stuff. Most of what I've learned has been from practical, hands-on experience. The more of that you can get, the better off you're going to be.

How many different jobs have you held in this field?

Five years after I graduated from technical school, I went back to teach basic electronics part time. The first time I lived in Nashville, I worked as chief technician for a tape duplication facility. I moved to Boston and supervised quality control for BASF (a manufacturer of recording tape) and then worked in their application engineering department. At that time I ran sound for a country band, and I also had a show on Boston's top country station. Then I moved back to Nashville to do marketing for BASF. I did a lot of freelance in between.

What do you currently do?

I service the technical needs of recording studios, tape duplication facilities and radio production facilities.

What do you like most about your work?

Being able to see a piece of equipment function again the way it was meant to and making it easy for the operator who has to use it. That gives me a good feeling. It makes me feel as though I'm using the gifts that were given to me.

What do you like least?

Making sure that I'm able to support my family. When I was working for somebody else exclusively, I didn't have such a good time because I knew that they were reaping the benefits of my efforts, and the payback wasn't there for me. That's why I made the choice to go out on my own. So there's a lot of pressure, but I wouldn't have it any other way.

What advice would you offer someone thinking about a career in technical maintenance?
Get in touch with someone who's in the business. See if that person can spend some time talking with you or allowing you to hang out while he works. See if it's something that you really want to do. The sooner you can make the decision about what career you want to follow, the better you can pursue the path and stick to it.

WHERE TO GO FROM HERE—SCHOOL INFORMATION

If you are interested in becoming a musician or singer, songwriter or composer, or in studying the academic side of music:

Courses in music theory and related topics are available at many high schools and most community colleges. Programs oriented toward commercial music and/or jazz are most helpful for aspiring professionals. Music schools and conservatories offer a variety of music courses, although their entrance requirements may be overly strict for musicians hoping to play rock, jazz, rap and other pop styles. A detailed listing of music programs in the U.S. and Canada can be found in *The Directory of Music Faculties* (CMS Publications, P.O. Box 8208, Missoula, Montana 59807-8202).

Instrumental performance is usually taught one-on-one with a private instructor. You can find qualified teachers in any music style through local offices of the American Federation of Musicians and through local music schools and college music departments in your area.

If you are interested in becoming a recording engineer or an audio maintenance technician or you want to learn more about the technology of recording:

Some community colleges and many recording studios, as well as schools that specialize in recording curricula, offer courses in computer literacy, MIDI technology, synthesis, audio recording and in related topics. Schools, seminars and programs are listed in *The Mix Master Directory of the Professional Audio Industry,* published by *Mix* magazine (P.O. Box 41094, Nashville, Tennessee 37204, phone 800-888-5139).

Two-year programs in electronics technology offered by community colleges and technical schools can provide a solid foundation for learning on the job. Get the *AES Education Directory*, which lists audio education programs. It's $6 from Audio Engineering Society (AES), 60 East 42nd Street, New York, New York 10165, phone 212-661-8528. The Association of Professional Audio Recording Studios (SPARS) publishes *New Ears*, a directory of audio education programs. It's available for $15 from SPARS, 4300 Tenth Avenue North, Lake Worth, Florida 33461, phone 407-461-6648.

If you are interested in becoming a musical equipment salesperson:

No formal educational programs exist, although manufacturers offer special seminars in operating and selling particularly complex pieces of gear. Music-related programs like those listed earlier for performers and technicians can contribute to an understanding of musicians, music-related equipment and the music business.

Courses in business-related subjects, available at any two- or four-year institution, may be helpful to those aiming for a management position. In addition, some schools offer courses specifically in the business of music. CMS Publications, Inc. (P.O. Box 8208, Missoula, Montana 59807-8202) publishes a directory of these programs.

USEFUL PUBLICATIONS

Pamphlets:

"Inside the Recording Industry: An Introduction to
America's Music Business"
free from:
The Recording Industry Association of American (RIAA)
1020 19th St. N.W. Suite 200
Washington, D.C. 20036
202-775-0101

Periodicals:

UL/Billboard
Subscription Dept.
P.O. Box 2011
Marion, Ohio 43306

Electronic Musician
Act III Publishing
P.O. Box 41094
Nashville, Tennessee 37204
800-888-5139, 615-377-3322

Guitar Player magazine
GPI/Miller-Freeman Publications
20085 Stevens Creek
Cupertino, California 95014
408-446-1105

Keyboard magazine
GPI/Miller-Freeman Publications
20085 Stevens Creek
Cupertino, California 95014

408-446-1105

Mix magazine
P.O. Box 41094
Nashville, Tennessee 37204
800-888-5139
Mix also publishes "The Mix Bookshelf Catalog," which lists useful books, videos and software. Call 800-233-9604 for your free copy.

Modern Drummer magazine
Attn: Subscriber Services
P.O. Box 480
Mount Morris, Illinois 61054-8079
800-435-0715

Musician magazine
1515 Broadway, 39th floor
New York, New York 10036
Attn: Subscription Dept.
212-536-5362
Musician publishes "The Musicians Guide to Touring and Promotion," a directory of record labels, radio stations, music publishers, nightclubs and other useful contacts ($5).

Books

Songwriter's Market
edited by Brian Rushing
Published by Writer's Digest Books

How to Make and Sell Your Own Record
by Diane Sward Rapaport
Published by Putnam Publishing Group

Handbook for Sound Engineers: The Audio Cyclopedia
by Glen Ballou
Published by Howard W. Sams & Company

The Musician's Home Recording Handbook
by Ted Greenwald
Published by GPI Books

This Business of Music and
More About This Business of Music
by Sidney Shemel and M. William Krasilovsky
Published by Watson-Guptil

WILL YOU FIT INTO THE WORLD OF MUSIC?

If a career as a musician or singer interests you, take this quiz:

Except in a few select niches such as playing sessions, the ingredients of a successful musical career don't follow any formula. What constitutes talent (not to mention good business sense) is highly subjective. Music history is full of stories of performers who were told to give it up and went on to greatness of one kind or another. The biggest successes seem to come from a combination of artistic vision, musical ability, good business sense and conditions far beyond anyone's control.

That said, most of the music industry survives on something less than large-scale success. In most cases, what counts is making sure people know who you are and what you do and being able to handle any opportunities that arise to play for pay (even if it means being the person who hires others to do the playing). This quiz is designed to reflect the demands of the workaday stratum of the musical world.

Read each statement, then choose the number 0, 5 or 10. The rating scale below explains what each number means.

> **0** = Disagree
> **5** = Agree somewhat
> **10** = Strongly agree

____I have a natural sense of rhythm, pitch and musical style

____I have the ability to produce a "demo," or demonstration recording, of my work

____I play an instrument or sing well, or I can hold an audience's attention on stage

___I'm capable of inventing my own musical parts

___I don't mind taking criticism and directions from others to improve my musical presentation

___I'm capable of organizing others to help me achieve my own career goals

___I'm capable of handling the promotional and financial aspects of my own career

___Making my living as a musician or singer is more important than having free time to spend with friends and family, a steady paycheck or a regular schedule

___I can improvise a musical part on the spot if I need to

___I have the discipline to practice and continually improve

Now add up your score.   ___Total points

If your total points are less than 50, you may want to reconsider your priorities or reevaluate your suitability for a career as an instrumentalist or singer. If your total points are between 50 and 75, you may have what it takes, but be sure to do more investigation. If your total points are 75 or more, it's likely that you're a good candidate for a career in musical performance.

If a career as a composer or songwriter interests you, take this quiz:

As with performers, there's no formula for success as a composer and/or songwriter. It depends on a number of unpredictable factors, among them subjective judgments made by people who may not share your musical values. In any particular musical style or market niche, it's relatively easy to tell whether or not the quality of your work is in the ball park. Still, in most cases, writing music requires a particular set of skills, talents and personality traits. The quiz lists a number of the most essential.

Read each statement, then choose the number 0, 5 or 10. The rating scale below explains what each number means.

> **0** = Disagree
> **5** = Agree somewhat
> **10** = Strongly agree

_____I like to come up with ideas for songs and/or musical compositions

_____I have the ability to imagine the sound I want and communicate it to others

_____I play an instrument and/or sing well enough to get my ideas across

_____I'm capable of directing other musicians to execute my ideas

_____I'm comfortable with synthesizers, sequencers and MIDI equipment, and with computers in general

_____I don't mind taking criticism and directions from others in order to improve my musical presentation

_____I like to work alone

_____I'm fascinated by the technical aspects of music, such as music theory, harmony, orchestration and notation

_____I'm capable of handling the promotional and financial aspects of my own career

_____A composing/songwriting career is more important to me than having free time to spend with friends and family, a steady paycheck or a regular schedule

Now add up your score.   _____Total points

If your total points are 50 or less, you may want to reconsider your priorities or reevaluate your suitability for a career as a composer or songwriter. If your total points are between 50 and 75, you may have what it takes, but be sure to do more investigation. If your total points are 75 or more, it's likely that you're a good candidate for a career in writing music.

If a career as a recording engineer interests you, take this quiz:

More than anything else, success as a recording engineer depends on your love for the environment and process of recording and your ability to face the stresses involved with a positive attitude. This quiz is designed to indicate how well suited you are in these areas.

Read each statement, then choose the number 0, 5 or 10. The rating scale below explains what each number means.

0 = Disagree

5 = Agree somewhat

10 = Strongly agree

___When I listen to music, I'm aware of the overall sound, as well as the details that contribute to it—not just the tune and the beat

___I'm fascinated by the process and technology of sound recording

___I'm comfortable with high-tech equipment, including computers

___I don't mind taking direction from others

___I'm willing to work long and unpredictable hours

___I know the sonic characteristics of various musical instruments and styles

___I have a natural sense of rhythm, pitch and musical style

___I feel I have the ability to assess the likely cause of a technical problem

___I can remain calm and productive in stressful situations

___I'm capable of concentrating and remaining seated for long periods of time

Now add up your score.   ___Total points

If your total points are 50 or less, you may want to reconsider your priorities or reevaluate your suitability for a career as a recording engineer. If your total points are between 50 and 75, you may have what it takes, but be sure to do more investigation. If your total points are 75 or more, it's likely that you're a good candidate to work in the field of recording engineering.

If a career as a musical equipment salesperson interests you, take this quiz:

Many frustrated musicians find great satisfaction in selling musical equipment. Success in sales demands a special combination of interpersonal skills, musical interest and motivation. This quiz identifies many of the most important factors.

Read each statement, then choose the number 0, 5 or 10. The rating scale below explains what each number means.

0 = Disagree
5 = Agree somewhat
10 = Strongly agree

___I play an instrument and/or sing fairly well

___I'm very outgoing and enjoy socializing with just about anybody

___The idea of asking people to buy from me doesn't make me uncomfortable

___I can handle rejection without taking it personally

___I'm comfortable working with numbers

___I have a good memory for facts and faces

___I'm fascinated by musical instruments, recording equipment and other music-related technology

___I'm comfortable with high-tech equipment, including computers

___I don't mind being on my feet for long periods of time

___I need the security of knowing that I can make a decent living in the music business

If your total points are 50 or less, you may want to reconsider your priorities or reevaluate your suitability for a career in musical equipment sales. If your total points are between 50 and 75, you may have what it takes, but be sure to do more investigation. If your total points are 75 or more, it's likely that you're a good candidate for work as a musical equipment salesperson.

If a career as an audio maintenance technician interests you, take this quiz:

This quiz identifies many of the most important skills, attitudes and personality traits necessary for success as an audio maintenance technician.

Read each statement, then choose the number 0, 5 or 10. The rating scale below explains what each number means.

0 = Disagree
5 = Agree somewhat
10 = Strongly agree

___I'm fascinated by the process and technology of sound recording

___I love electronics and high-tech devices

___I'm a tinkerer; I like to find out how things work

___I'm comfortable with technical subjects and the sciences

___I have experience using basic machine shop tools (such as a drill) and basic electronics tools (such as a soldering iron, a volt/ohm meter and an oscilloscope), or I would like to learn how

___I'm good at problem solving and logic

___I'm an organized, methodical type of person

___I work well under pressure

___I don't mind staying behind the scenes

___I understand basic electronics—analog and digital—or am willing to learn

Now add up your score.   ___Total points

If your total points are 50 or less, you may want to reconsider your priorities or reevaluate your suitability for a career in technical maintenance. If your total points are between 50 and 75, you may have what it takes to be an audio maintenance technician, but be sure to do more investigation. If your total points are 75 or more, it's likely that you're a good candidate to work in this field.

Keep in mind that the music industry offers numerous other career options as well, and that new ones are developing all the time. If you don't imagine yourself in one of the five careers featured in this book, consider looking into other possibilities. For more information, consult the book *Career Opportunities in the Music Industry* by Shelly Field (published by Facts on File).

ABOUT THE AUTHOR

Ted Greenwald lives in New York, where he divides his time between writing and composing. His music can be heard on the albums *Soul of the Machine: The Windham Hill Sampler of Electronic Music* and *Views from a Distance*, with Scott Hiltzik, on Sonic Atmospheres Records. He has also contributed music to television and radio commercials for Southern Bell, Brut, Comedy Central Cable Network and others and has worked on the engineering staff at Power Station Recording Studios in New York.

Greenwald is the author of *The Rock and Roll Companion*, *The Beatles Companion*, and *The Musician's Home Recording Guide*. A nationally recognized authority on recording, synthesizers and sequencing, he contributes regularly to *Keyboard*, *Guitar Player*, *EQ* and *Creem*.